country home
cooking & crafts

Publications International, Ltd.

Favorite Brand Name Recipes at www.fbnr.com

ISBN: 0-7853-6680-6

Library of Congress Control Number: 2002100168

Manufactured in China.

8 7 6 5 4 3 2 1

Contents

Herbed White Bread

Herbes de Provence, a blend of dried herbs typical of southern French cooking, can be purchased separately or you can find jars of premixed herbes de Provence in most supermarkets. If using the latter, you will need 10 tablespoons or about 6 ounces. Be aware, however, that the mixture varies from company to company, sometimes containing lavender, which is not recommended for this bread. So check the contents listed on the label.

What You'll Need

- 4 cups all-purpose flour
- 1 cake (0.6 ounce) fresh yeast
- ½ teaspoon sugar
- 6 tablespoons warm milk
- 2 onions, peeled and chopped
- 4½ teaspoons vegetable oil
- 4 tablespoons dried oregano
- 4 tablespoons dried thyme
- 1 tablespoon dried rosemary
- 1 tablespoon dried savory
- ½ teaspoon freshly ground black pepper
- Pinch of freshly grated nutmeg
- 1 egg yolk, lightly beaten

1. Sift 2½ cups flour into bowl. Make well in center. Crumble yeast into well. Add sugar and warm milk.

2. Using mixer with kneading attachment or dough hook, knead until blended. Cover; let rise in warm, draft-free place 15 minutes.

3. Knead dough, adding enough warm water and remaining 1½ cups flour to make smooth dough.

4. Cover; let rise in warm, draft-free place 15 minutes. In skillet, sauté chopped onions in oil until golden; cool. Preheat oven to 350°F. Lightly grease 9-inch loaf pan.

5. Add onions, dried herbs, and spices to dough; with hands, knead until evenly distributed.

6. Fit dough into prepared pan. Slash top; brush with yolk. Bake 40 to 45 minutes or until loaf sounds hollow when tapped. Cool on wire rack.

Makes 1 loaf

Cherry Coffee Cake

For this luscious coffee cake, a tender yeast dough flavored with lemon peel is rolled out, sprinkled with milk, and topped with tart red cherries and crumbly cinnamon-spiked streusel. It takes 50 minutes to rise and about 30 minutes to bake, but it is worth the time. Serve it for breakfast with coffee, as a snack with afternoon tea, or as an informal dessert. To cut back on preparation time, use a standing mixer with a dough hook to knead the dough.

What You'll Need

Cake

- 3 cups all-purpose flour
- 1 cake (0.6 ounce) fresh yeast
- 1 cup warm milk
- 7 tablespoons unsalted butter, cut into pieces
- 1 egg
- Pinch of salt
- ½ teaspoon grated lemon peel

Streusel

- 1½ cups all-purpose flour
- 10 tablespoons unsalted butter, cut into pieces
- ½ cup sugar
- 1 teaspoon ground cinnamon

Topping

- ¼ cup whole milk
- ½ teaspoon vanilla extract
- 1 jar (16 ounces) pitted sour red cherries or ¾ pound fresh cherries, pitted

1. Sift flour into large mixing bowl. Make well in center of flour; crumble yeast into well.

2. Pour milk into yeast; stir together, incorporating some of the flour. Cover bowl; let rise for 20 minutes.

3. Add butter, egg, salt, and lemon peel; knead until well blended. Cover; let rise for 20 minutes. Combine streusel ingredients until crumbly.

4. Grease 17×12-inch baking pan. On lightly floured surface, roll out dough to fit pan.

5. Fit dough into prepared pan. For topping, combine milk and vanilla; brush over dough. Sprinkle dough evenly with cherries and streusel. Preheat oven to 350°F.

6. Let cake rise for 10 minutes. Bake for 30 to 35 minutes. Cool slightly; cut on diagonal to form diamonds.

Makes 1 coffee cake

Raspberry Muffins

Muffin pans come in a variety of shapes and sizes. For this recipe, use a standard-size pan. To ease the removal of the baked muffins from the pan, you can line the cups with special paper liners, or simply grease them. For even baking, fill any empty cups with water. It is important to stir the batter quickly just until the ingredients are moistened. Overmixing will mash the raspberries and produce flat, tough muffins.

What You'll Need

- ¼ cup quick-cooking oatmeal
- 1 cup buttermilk
- 1 egg
- ½ cup sugar
- ⅓ cup vegetable oil
- 2 cups all-purpose flour
- 1 tablespoon baking powder
- 1 teaspoon ground cinnamon
- 1 cup fresh raspberries

1. Preheat oven to 400°F. In medium bowl, combine oatmeal and buttermilk; set aside 10 minutes to allow oatmeal to expand.

2. Lightly beat egg. Add egg, sugar, and oil to oatmeal mixture; stir to combine.

3. Mix flour, baking powder, and cinnamon. Sift over oatmeal mixture and stir until just combined.

4. Pick over raspberries; wash then pat them dry with paper towels. Add to batter and mix gently.

5. Prepare standard-size muffin pan cups: Insert paper baking liners into muffin cups, or lightly grease muffin cups.

6. Fill cups two-thirds full, and bake on middle rack of oven for 25 minutes. Cool slightly.
Makes 1 dozen muffins

Braided Bread Wreath

The tantalizing aroma and full-bodied flavor of home-baked bread can be enjoyed on a regular basis. While yeast breads require additional time for a lot of kneading and rising, this hearty onion-laden bread is leavened with baking powder, which allows it to go straight into the oven after it is braided into a wreath and sprinkled with sesame, poppy, and sunflower seeds. This delicious bread can be baked the day before and reheated in a 250°F oven just before serving.

What You'll Need

- 6 tablespoons olive oil, divided
- 1 medium onion, chopped
- 2/3 cup cottage cheese
- 1/2 cup whole milk
- 1 whole egg
- 1 tablespoon salt
- 4 cups all-purpose flour
- 4 teaspoons baking powder
- 1 egg yolk
- 1 teaspoon water
- 2 tablespoons sesame seeds
- 2 tablespoons poppy seeds
- 2 tablespoons sunflower seeds

1. Heat 1 tablespoon olive oil in skillet over medium heat. Add onion and sauté until deep golden; cool. Combine cottage cheese, milk, whole egg, salt, remaining 5 tablespoons olive oil, and sautéed onion in large bowl; mix well.

2. Whisk together flour and baking powder. Sift mixture over wet ingredients and stir to combine until dough forms.

3. Knead dough on lightly floured surface with floured hands until smooth and shiny.

4. Preheat oven to 350°F. Line baking sheet with parchment. Divide dough into thirds. Roll each piece into 2-foot length. Braid lengths together. Place on prepared baking sheet.

5. Form braid into wreath, pressing ends together firmly. Bake for 30 minutes.

6. Lightly beat yolk with water; brush over wreath and sprinkle with seeds. Bake another 15 minutes or until bread sounds hollow when tapped.
Makes 1 (2-pound) wreath

Cinnamon Danish Swirls

*C*risp on the outside, soft and chewy on the inside, these golden sweet buns need no extras. What makes them so special is a butter-rich Danish yeast dough created by rolling chilled pieces of butter into the dough, then folding the dough over, rolling out the dough, and repeating the process. Brushed with melted butter and sprinkled with cinnamon-sugar, the dough is finally rolled up, cut into pieces, and baked until fragrant. A marvelous dessert, they are also perfect for breakfast.

What You'll Need

- 10 tablespoons unsalted butter, softened
- 4 cups all-purpose flour, divided
- ½ cup sugar, divided
- 2 teaspoons ground cinnamon
- 1 cake (0.6 ounce) fresh yeast
- 1 teaspoon salt
- 1 cup warm water
- 5 tablespoons butter, melted and cooled

1. Knead softened butter with ⅓ cup flour until well blended. Shape into log, wrap in foil; chill. Mix ¼ cup sugar and cinnamon; set aside.

2. Combine remaining 3⅔ cups flour, yeast, remaining ¼ cup sugar, salt, and warm water until soft dough forms. Roll dough to form 16×12-inch rectangle.

3. Cut ⅓ of chilled butter crosswise into thin slices and arrange in single layer, slightly overlapping on bottom half of dough rectangle.

4. Fold top ½ down, over butter; press. Fold bottom ⅓ up and top ⅓ down, overlapping bottom ⅓. Cover; chill 30 minutes. Roll on floured surface until doubled. Turn 90°; repeat **3** and **4** twice.

5. Preheat oven to 400°F. Roll dough to 24×12 inches. Brush with melted butter. Sprinkle with cinnamon-sugar.

6. From long end, roll up dough. Cut into 16 pieces; place, cut-side up, on baking sheet lined with parchment; bake 15 to 20 minutes.   *Makes 16 buns*

Hearty Banana Bread

*F*ast and easy, quick bread is a baker's best friend. For the best flavor in this bread, use very ripe bananas and make sure that all the ingredients are at room temperature. A treat for breakfast, this bread is also excellent with afternoon tea or coffee or with a small scoop of vanilla ice cream for dessert.

What You'll Need

- **10 tablespoons unsalted butter, softened**
- **⅓ cup honey**
- **Pinch of salt**
- **4 ripe medium bananas, divided**
- **4 eggs**
- **2 cups whole-wheat flour**
- **2 teaspoons baking powder**
- **½ cup chopped toasted walnuts**
- **Juice of ½ lemon**
- **½ cup walnut halves**
- **2 tablespoons honey, warmed**

1. Preheat oven to 400°F. Grease bottom only of 10-inch loaf pan. Beat butter, honey, and salt until creamy. Peel and mash 2 bananas; stir into butter mixture.

2. Add eggs to mixture, 1 at a time, whisking after each addition. Sift flour with baking powder.

3. Gradually stir flour mixture into butter mixture, until mixed. Fold in chopped walnuts. Peel and slice remaining 2 bananas; toss with lemon juice.

4. Pour batter into prepared pan; smooth top.

5. Arrange banana slices, overlapping, in 2 rows across top of batter. Bake on middle rack of oven for 40 minutes.

6. Place walnut halves between bananas; bake 10 minutes. Cool 5 minutes; run thin-bladed knife around sides of pan. Tip pan to remove loaf. Drizzle with warmed honey. Cool on wire rack. Wrap in foil; let stand 24 hours before serving.

Makes 1 (10-inch) loaf

Pull-Apart Seeded Rolls

*N*othing complements a meal like freshly baked bread, especially when it comes in the form of easy-to-serve yeast rolls that feature two different seeded toppings. The yeast dough, enriched with butter and egg yolk, is kneaded, left to rise, then shaped into rolls, which are placed close together in a round baking pan. After a final rising, the rolls are brushed with egg, then sprinkled with either caraway or sesame seeds. As the basket is passed, diners can pull apart their roll of choice.

What You'll Need

- **3 cups all-purpose flour**
- **1 ounce fresh yeast**
- **Pinch of sugar**
- **1/2 teaspoon salt**
- **3/4 cup milk, warmed and divided**
- **9 tablespoons unsalted butter, melted and cooled**
- **1 egg yolk**
- **1 whole egg, lightly beaten**
- **3 to 4 tablespoons caraway seeds**
- **2 tablespoons sesame seeds**

1. Sift flour into mixing bowl; make well in center. Crumble yeast into well.

2. Sprinkle sugar over yeast; sprinkle salt around edges of flour. Add 1/4 cup milk and some flour to yeast in well.

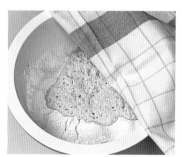

3. Cover bowl and set aside in warm, draft-free place for 5 to 10 minutes or until yeast mixture begins to foam.

4. Stir in 1/2 cup milk, butter, and egg yolk; knead until dough forms. Cover; let rise in warm, draft-free place 30 minutes.

5. Knead dough; shape into 18-inch log on floured surface. Cut into 1 1/2-inch slices; form into balls. Place in greased pie plate, first around edge, then in middle. Brush with whole egg.

6. Sprinkle rolls with seeds as shown. Cover; let rise in warm, draft-free place 15 minutes. Bake in preheated 400°F oven 40 minutes. *Makes 12 rolls*

Blueberry Crêpes

rêpes are adored by adults and children all over the world. These French pancakes can be filled or topped with sweet or savory fillings. To prevent lumps in the batter, stir the milk and the egg mixture into the flour, not the other way around. For this recipe a crêpe pan is used. An ordinary frying pan will work equally well, however, instead of the pan lid, use a spatula to turn the crêpes. Keep the pan lightly coated with the butter/oil mixture; wipe the pan with a paper towel after cooking each crêpe.

What You'll Need

- 4 eggs
- Pinch of salt
- ¼ cup sugar
- 1 teaspoon vanilla extract
- ¾ cup all-purpose flour
- 1¼ cups milk
- 3 tablespoons butter
- 3 tablespoons sunflower oil
- 1½ cups fresh blueberries, washed and stemmed
- Confectioners' sugar

1. In bowl, whisk eggs, salt, sugar, and vanilla until well blended. Sift flour into separate mixing bowl.

2. Add milk to flour; whisk to combine. Gradually add egg mixture and whisk until smooth.

3. Heat some butter and oil in equal amounts in pan. Ladle batter into pan; tip pan back and forth to spread evenly.

4. Distribute blueberries as abundantly as desired onto the batter; fry until bottom of crêpe is golden.

5. Slide crêpe onto lid of pan, right-side up. With paper towel, wipe out pan; moisten pan with more butter and oil.

6. Place pan over lid; flip crêpe upside down. Slide back into pan. Finish frying opposite side. Place crêpe on serving plate; sprinkle with confectioners' sugar; serve warm.

Makes 6 to 8 crêpes

Braided Onion-Garlic Bread

A loaf of home-baked bread makes the perfect accompaniment to any quick lunch or hearty dinner. For a beautiful, shiny crust, simply sprinkle this braid with water just before putting it in the oven and again 5 minutes before taking it out. To make an impressive host or hostess gift, wrap the cooled bread in clear or colored plastic wrap and tie it with a decorative bow.

What You'll Need

- 2 cups all-purpose flour
- ⅔ ounce fresh yeast
- 2 tablespoons whole milk
- 1 tablespoon sugar
- 3 tablespoons butter
- 3 onions, diced
- 3 cloves garlic, minced
- ½ cup warm water
- 2 to 3 tablespoons oil
- 1 tablespoon salt

1. Pour flour into large bowl. Make well in center; crumble yeast into well. Mix in milk and sugar. Cover; let rise in warm, draft-free place 15 minutes.

2. Melt butter in skillet over medium heat; sauté onions until golden. Stir in garlic.

3. Add water, oil, and salt to dough; knead until well blended and dough is smooth and shiny.

4. Spread onion mixture over dough and knead until evenly distributed. Cover and let rise in warm, draft-free place for 15 minutes. Grease large baking sheet.

5. Divide dough into 3 equal pieces; roll into 3 ropes of equal length. Preheat oven to 350°F.

6. Braid ropes. Place on baking sheet; let rise in warm, draft-free place 10 minutes. Sprinkle with water; bake 25 minutes or until loaf sounds hollow when tapped.
Makes 1 loaf

Powdered Jelly Donuts

For tender donuts, the dough must be soft, not stiff as if making bread. Work the dough on a well-floured work surface and make sure the oil's temperature is 375°F. If the temperature is too high, the donuts will cook on the outside and not on the inside; if the temperature is too low, they'll absorb fat and will taste greasy.

What You'll Need

- 1½ ounces fresh yeast
- 1 cup milk, warmed
- ½ cup sugar, divided
- 4 cups all-purpose flour, divided
- ½ cup (1 stick) butter, melted
- 2 egg yolks
- 2 pinches of salt
- Apricot jam
- Vegetable oil or fat for frying
- ⅔ cup confectioners' sugar

1. Crumble yeast into large mixing bowl. Add warm milk, 1 teaspoon sugar, and 1 cup flour; stir to combine.

2. Cover starter; place in warm, draft-free place and let rise for 15 minutes, or until doubled in size.

3. Add butter, egg yolks, remaining sugar, and salt to starter; knead until soft dough forms. Cover and let rise for 45 minutes, or until doubled in size.

4. On floured surface, roll dough ¾ inch thick. Use cup or biscuit cutter to cut 48 rounds.

5. Spoon 1 teaspoon jam onto middle of 24 rounds; top with remaining rounds. Press edges.

6. Pour 2 inches oil into large, deep skillet. Heat over medium heat until deep-fry thermometer registers 375°F. Adjust heat to maintain temperature. Fry donuts 4 minutes per side. Place on paper towel-lined wire rack; cool. Dust with confectioners' sugar.   *Makes 24 donuts*

Viennese-Style Fried Chicken

*F*or this recipe, use a heavy
metal pan that conducts
heat well. Preheating the pan
before adding the oil helps
prevent the chicken from
sticking to the pan. Chilling
the coated chicken allows the
chicken to absorb the flavors
and helps the coating adhere.
For a very crispy coating, fry
the chicken only until
browned, then finish cooking
it in a preheated 350°F oven.

What You'll Need

- **1 chicken (about 3½ pounds)**
- **Salt**
- **2 eggs**
- **3 tablespoons whole milk**
- **4 tablespoons all-purpose flour**
- **½ cup bread crumbs**
- **Fresh vegetable oil**
- **1 bunch fresh parsley, washed, patted dry, and trimmed**
- **1 lemon, cut into 8 wedges**

1. Cut chicken into 8 pieces; wash under cold running water and pat dry with paper towels.

2. Rub salt (and any additional desired seasonings) on chicken pieces. In shallow bowl, beat eggs and milk with fork.

3. Spread flour and bread crumbs on separate plates.

4. Coat chicken in flour, then egg, and then bread crumbs. Press to adhere. Place chicken on plate; cover and let rest in refrigerator 15 to 20 minutes.

5. Heat oil in heavy skillet over medium heat until hot. Fry chicken just until bubbles form on top. Turn; fry until golden.

6. Drain chicken on paper towels. Fry parsley in bunches until crispy. Serve chicken with parsley, lemon wedges, and potato salad, if desired.

Makes 4 servings

Potatoes Au Gratin

O nce you have tasted this rich, hearty potato casserole, you'll want to serve it as often as possible. For the best consistency, use starchy, mealy potatoes, such as Idaho or all-purpose white potatoes with brown skins. Peel the potatoes, then slice them ¼ inch thick. If the slices are too thick or too thin, they will not absorb the cream and cheese properly. This recipe calls for Emmentaler cheese, a semifirm cheese from Switzerland, but you can substitute equal amounts of Swiss or Gruyère.

What You'll Need

1½ **pounds all-purpose white potatoes (about 4 or 5)**

8 **ounces Emmentaler cheese**

1 **tablespoon butter**

1 **clove garlic**

Salt and black pepper to taste

¼ **teaspoon grated nutmeg**

1 **cup plain yogurt (whole milk)**

2 **cups crème fraîche or heavy cream**

1. Wash and peel potatoes; cut into ¼-inch-thick slices with sharp knife. Finely grate cheese.

2. Preheat oven to 350°F. Butter shallow ovenproof ceramic baking dish. Peel and press or mince garlic; spread evenly on bottom of dish.

3. Arrange one layer of potato slices evenly in baking dish. Season with salt, pepper, and nutmeg.

4. In bowl, combine yogurt and crème fraîche or heavy cream; spoon one-third mixture evenly over potatoes.

5. Continue to layer with potatoes, seasonings, and yogurt mixture, finishing with yogurt mixture.

6. Sprinkle grated cheese liberally over yogurt layer. Bake, uncovered, 45 to 50 minutes or until top is golden brown and crusty.

Makes 4 to 6 servings

Zucchini & Carrot Fritters

*Z*ucchini pancakes are a great way to use a bumper crop of squash from your garden. Look for smaller, young, blemish-free zucchini; because the skin is sweet, they need not be peeled. The grated zucchini must be salted, drained, and pressed in a sieve in order to remove excess water; otherwise, the pancakes will not hold together when fried. Garnish these tasty pancakes with cherry tomatoes and mint leaves, if desired.

What You'll Need

- 3 medium zucchini (about 1 pound)
- Salt
- 2 to 3 medium carrots (about ⅔ pound)
- 2 scallions
- 3 tablespoons chopped fresh parsley
- 3 tablespoons chopped fresh dill
- 3 eggs
- ¼ cup all-purpose flour
- Freshly ground black pepper
- Pinch of ground coriander
- 2 tablespoons vegetable oil

1. Wash zucchini; pat dry. Trim ends; scrape brown spots. With hand grater, coarsely grate zucchini into large bowl.

4. Wash scallions thoroughly; trim beards and leaves; slice white portions into thin rings. Add to grated vegetables.

2. Sprinkle grated zucchini liberally with salt; let stand for at least 15 minutes. Peel carrots; grate into another bowl.

5. Add herbs, eggs, and flour to grated vegetables; combine thoroughly. Season to taste with salt, pepper, and coriander.

3. Drain zucchini over sieve, pressing gently with back of spoon to extract excess water. Add to grated carrots.

6. In skillet, heat oil until very hot. For each fritter, spoon 2 tablespoons batter into skillet. Flatten into 3-inch pancake; fry about 5 minutes or until golden, turning once. Serve hot.

Makes about 8 (3-inch) fritters

Herbed Pork Roast

Your guests will rave when you serve this delicious, elegant roast. Serve it warm with mashed potatoes and gravy for a hearty meal or wonderful buffet. Or, serve this pork roast cold with tossed salad and crusty bread for a fabulous picnic spread.

What You'll Need

- 1 (3-pound) boneless pork loin roast, all gristle removed
- Salt
- Freshly ground black pepper
- 6 sprigs fresh basil
- 4 sprigs fresh oregano
- 4 sprigs fresh thyme
- 3 sprigs fresh rosemary
- 5 leaves fresh sage
- 3 cloves garlic, minced
- 3 tablespoons fresh lemon juice
- ¼ cup olive oil
- 1¼ cups water or white wine

1. Place meat flat on work surface. With mallet, pound to even thickness. Season with salt and pepper.

2. Wash herbs and pat dry. Remove leaves from stems, as necessary; finely chop.

3. Mix garlic, chopped herbs, lemon juice and olive oil into paste; spread two-thirds of mixture over meat.

4. From long side, roll up meat tightly; secure with kitchen twine. Rub remaining herb paste over roast.

5. Wrap meat; chill 2 hours. Preheat oven to 425°F. Unwrap meat; place in roasting pan. Add water. Bake 15 minutes. Reduce oven temperature to 350°F. Tent roast with foil; bake, turning occasionally, 1 hour 15 minutes.

6. Remove from oven; discard twine. Let roast rest 15 minutes before cutting into thin slices.
Makes 8 to 10 servings

Watermelon Fruit Bowl

*S*afely cut the watermelon rind into the spiked design with a very sharp, heavy-bladed knife of medium length. Remove the flesh from the melon; pat the shell dry with paper towels, and keep it chilled until you are ready to fill it. For the best flavor, make the fruit salad, leaving out the strawberries, the night before you wish to serve it; cover and refrigerate. Allow at least 30 minutes for the fruit to come to room temperature, then add the strawberries (this preserves their wonderful color) and serve.

What You'll Need

- **1 watermelon (about 5 pounds)**
- **½ pound green grapes, washed and patted dry**
- **½ pound red grapes, washed and patted dry**
- **2 nectarines**
- **½ pound strawberries, washed and patted dry**
- **4 tablespoons fresh lemon juice**
- **1 tablespoon orange liqueur**
- **Mint leaves for garnish (optional)**

1. With nontoxic marker, draw spiked design on rind one-third of length from one end of watermelon.

4. Halve grapes; remove seeds. Halve and pit nectarines; cut into slices. Hull and halve strawberries.

2. With very sharp knife, carefully cut out spiked design, neatly following marked pattern.

5. In bowl, combine fruit, including melon balls. Toss with lemon juice and orange liqueur. Marinate 2 to 3 hours.

3. Using melon baller, scoop out flesh from melon, including top section, removing as many seeds as possible.

6. Gently toss fruit and their juices, then spoon into watermelon shell. Garnish with mint leaves, if desired.

Makes 6 servings

All-American Chicken Sandwich

s chicken has become more popular as a main course, so too, have its versatile leftovers. One way to utilize this bounty is to make chicken salad. Instead of a standard sandwich, make a double-decker with two kinds of bread, lettuce and tomato, and a blend of chicken, crispy vegetables and fresh herbs. Deck out a platter of these club sandwiches with fancy toothpicks to serve at your next party, or bring some along to a friend's house for lunch or afternoon tea.

What You'll Need

- 2 **ribs celery**
- 2 **scallions**
- 1 **small carrot**
- ¼ **cucumber**
- 1 **small tomato**
- 4 **ounces cooked boneless skinless chicken breast**
- ¼ **cup mayonnaise**
- 1 **tablespoon chopped fresh parsley**
- 1 **tablespoon chopped fresh chives**
- **Salt and black pepper to taste**
- 8 **slices multigrain bread**
- 4 **slices bread of desired type**
- 8 **lettuce leaves**
- 8 **tomato slices**
- 16 **decorative toothpicks**

1. Wash and dry celery, scallions, carrot, cucumber, and tomato; finely chop. Cut chicken into small cubes.

2. Mix chopped vegetables, cubed chicken, and mayonnaise. Stir in parsley and chives; season with salt and pepper.

3. Toast 8 slices multigrain bread and 4 slices bread of contrasting type. Let toast cool.

4. Top each of 4 slices multigrain toast with 1 lettuce leaf, 1 tomato slice, and one-eighth of chicken salad.

5. Top each with 1 slice contrasting toast, remaining chicken salad, 1 lettuce leaf, and 1 tomato slice.

6. Top each with 1 slice of remaining multigrain toast. Cut sandwiches diagonally into 4 triangles. Insert decorative toothpick into each quarter.
Makes 4 sandwiches

Basket-Weave Potato Chips

The best oils for deep-frying are canola, corn, peanut, safflower, and soy. Never fill the pan more than half full of oil, and heat the oil gradually to avoid spattering of any moisture. The temperature of the oil, 375°F, is critical for a crisp exterior and delicious interior. When using a deep-fat thermometer, make sure the bulb is completely immersed in the oil but not touching the bottom of the pan. If you don't have a thermometer, drop in a 1-inch cube of bread; it should take about 1 minute to brown when the temperature of the oil is correct.

What You'll Need

6 unblemished firm well-shaped Idaho potatoes

Oil for frying

2 pounds (4 cups) deep-frying fat

1 teaspoon paprika

1 teaspoon salt

1. Wash potatoes well under cold running water.

2. Peel potatoes and remove any eyes. Wash again and pat dry. Fill heavy pan half full with oil and gradually heat to 375°F.

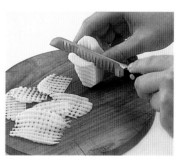

3. For basket-weave slices, using crinkle cutter, cut potato very thinly crosswise, then rotate and cut lengthwise.

4. When oil has reached 375°F, add potato chips 1 at a time; fry until just golden brown, about 1 minute.

5. Using spatula or slotted spoon, remove potato chips from oil 1 at a time. Drain on paper towels.

6. When fully drained, place potato chips in attractive serving bowl and season to taste with paprika and salt.

Makes 4 servings

Sweet & Spicy Beet Salad

Fresh beets, available year-round, should be firm and smooth when purchased. Small and medium-size beets are the most tender. Cooked beets are easy to peel if cooled and held under cold running water. Beets will stain your hands (as well as wooden or plastic utensils), so always wear disposable rubber gloves when handling them. Mâche, also called corn salad, field salad, or lamb's lettuce, is a spoon-shaped green with a tangy, nutty flavor. It does not keep well, so use it within a day or two of purchase.

What You'll Need

- **2 pounds small red beets**
- **4 ounces mâche**
- **2 cloves garlic**
- **5 tablespoons olive oil**
- **3 to 4 tablespoons white wine vinegar**
- **Salt and black pepper to taste**
- **⅛ teaspoon ground coriander**
- **½ cup coarsely chopped toasted walnuts**

1. Wash beets carefully, without piercing skin. Cover with water; boil until tender, 30 to 40 minutes.

4. Wearing rubber gloves, peel cooked beets and slice thinly with sharp knife or with crinkle cutter, if desired.

2. Drain beets, reserving cooking liquid; let cool. Pour 5 tablespoons of liquid into bowl for dressing.

5. In bowl, whisk olive oil, vinegar, salt, pepper, and coriander into 5 tablespoons cooking liquid until blended.

3. Wash mâche; trim as necessary and pat dry. Arrange on individual plates. Peel and mince garlic.

6. Arrange beets on top of mâche; sprinkle with minced garlic and walnuts. Spoon on dressing; serve immediately.

Makes 4 servings

Delicious Herbed Butter

For rich taste and creamy smooth texture, butter has no equal, and an herbed, or "composed," butter will be one of the most effective and versatile flavor enhancers in your culinary repertoire. To give as a gift, shape the butter into a smooth cylinder by pressing gently and rolling it back and forth between 2 sheets of foil. Wrap the butter in foil, chill it until very firm, and then give it wrapped in paper. Make sure that you include the instructions for refrigerating the butter.

What You'll Need

1½ **sticks unsalted butter, softened**

1 **smooth unblemished lemon**

Fresh chives

½ **teaspoon black peppercorns**

1. Cut butter into small pieces. Using whisk or electric mixer, beat until fluffy.

2. Clean lemon with brush and rinse thoroughly under hot running water. Grate peel and squeeze juice.

3. Rinse chives and pat dry with paper towels. On cutting board, using chef's knife, finely chop chives to make about 2 tablespoons.

4. Place peppercorns in mortar. Using pestle, grind peppercorns against bottom and side of mortar until fine.

5. Add lemon peel, lemon juice, chives, and pepper to butter; stir until blended. Spoon into rectangular container and chill at least 4 hours.

6. To serve, cut butter into slices, then cube. Using melon baller, make some butter balls.

Makes 6 ounces

Summery Chicken Salad

We're always on the lookout for light, healthful, protein-rich dishes that are easy to prepare, especially those in which we can use up our leftovers. Made of peas, beans, and lean, roasted chicken breast, all dressed in a tangy vinaigrette, this salad could not be more in tune with today's healthier low-calorie, low-fat lifestyle. Not only is it a perfect warm-weather luncheon dish, it's also a lively addition to any cold buffet and is ideal for parties. You'll be surprised by how easy it is to make!

What You'll Need

- **10 ounces frozen peas**
- **10 ounces frozen green beans**
- **1 pound roasted chicken breast**
- **1 small onion**
- **3 tablespoons white wine vinegar**
- **1 teaspoon sugar**
- **1 teaspoon tangy mustard**
- **½ teaspoon salt**
- **½ teaspoon prepared horseradish**
- **¼ teaspoon white pepper**
- **4 tablespoons olive oil**
- **1 head Boston or butter lettuce**

1. Defrost peas and green beans. Blanch in boiling salted water 4 minutes. Transfer vegetables to strainer. Place strainer under cold running water; drain well.

2. Cut skinned, boned chicken breast into small cubes. Chill until ready to add to vegetable mixture.

3. Peel onion. On cutting board, using a sharp knife, cut onion in half lengthwise through root end; finely chop both onion halves.

4. Mix onion, 2 tablespoons vinegar, sugar, mustard, salt, horseradish, and pepper. Add olive oil; whisk until thickened.

5. Add chicken to vegetables; toss to combine. Add remaining 1 tablespoon vinegar; toss to coat. Refrigerate 30 minutes.

6. Wash Boston lettuce and pat dry with paper towels. Line salad bowls with lettuce. Top with chicken mixture.
Makes 4 side-dish or appetizer servings

Pickled Summer Vegetables

When preparing this recipe, use a nonmetallic bowl and utensils to avoid a reaction with the vinegar. Pickling, sea, and kosher salts are free of any additives that would cloud the brine. Do not overfill the jars; leave room for the vinegar to surround the vegetables. Check the jars 1 or 2 days after sealing; if necessary, add more vinegar to cover the vegetables completely. Stored in a cool, dry, well-ventilated place, the pickled vegetables will keep about 8 months.

What You'll Need

- 1 small cauliflower
- ½ pound green beans
- 8 small carrots
- 16 scallions
- 2 red bell peppers
- 2 yellow bell peppers
- 4 green chili peppers
- 7 (1-pint) sterilized widemouthed glass jars with tight-fitting lids
- 7 cloves garlic
- 7 sprigs fresh dill
- 1 quart white wine vinegar
- 1 quart water
- ¾ cup pickling, sea, or kosher salt

1. Wash cauliflower and separate into florets. Wash and trim green beans; cut into 2-inch lengths.

2. Peel and slice carrots, using crinkle cutter, if desired. Wash and trim scallions; cut crosswise into quarters.

3. Wash peppers; halve, core, and seed bell peppers. Cut bell peppers into strips. Seed chili peppers and cut into rings.

4. Mix cut vegetables in large bowl; divide among 7 (1-pint) sterilized jars, or layer in jars by type.

5. Peel garlic. Wash dill and pat dry. Add 1 clove garlic and 1 sprig dill to each jar.

6. Bring vinegar, water, and salt to a boil; pour over vegetables, covering by at least ½ inch. Tap jars; seal. Keep in cool, dark place at least 4 weeks.

Makes 7 (1-pint) jars

Peppered Apple Rings

A pples, perhaps the most popular of all fruits, are at their best from September through November, but can be enjoyed well after their peak season once they have been preserved. Tart, firm apples, such as pippin, Granny Smith, Cortland, Rome Beauty, and Baldwin, are best for preserving this way. The apple rings will keep for about 2 to 3 months in a cool, dark place; refrigerate them after opening. Serve these piquant rings with a cheese plate or use them to enliven ham, roast pork, turkey, or game.

2 pounds tart apples

1 pound green bell peppers

3 (1-pint) sterilized widemouthed glass jars with tight-fitting lids

3 tablespoons juniper berries

1 quart apple cider vinegar

¾ cup sugar

1 tablespoon peppercorns

4 teaspoons salt

1. Choose firm, unblemished apples. Peel apples; remove cores with apple corer.

2. Cut apples crosswise into rings. Wash bell peppers and pat dry. Remove stems, seeds, and white ribs from peppers.

3. Cut bell peppers into even strips. In sterilized glass jar, loosely pack alternating layers of apple rings and bell pepper strips.

4. Sprinkle juniper berries over top. In nonreactive pot, bring vinegar, sugar, peppercorns, and salt to a boil, stirring constantly.

5. Place jar on damp kitchen cloth. Pour hot vinegar into jars, covering contents and filling almost to top. Tap jar to release air bubbles.

6. Wipe rim with clean, damp cloth; secure lid. Let stand for 2 to 3 weeks in cool, dark place before serving. Decorate jar for gift-giving, if desired.
Makes about 3 (1-pint) jars

Fried Herbed Chicken

For this recipe, if you are using frozen chicken breasts, make sure they are fully thawed before coating them. Letting the chicken breasts rest in the refrigerator after they are coated allows the chicken to absorb all the flavors and will make the coating adhere better when fried. To check the doneness of the chicken, prick the breast in the thickest part with a skewer or the point of a sharp knife; if the juices that run out are clear, the chicken is done.

What You'll Need

- 4 **boneless skinless chicken breast halves**
- 1 **egg yolk, lightly beaten**
- 2 **tablespoons Dijon mustard**
- 3 **tablespoons heavy cream**
- 4 **tablespoons chopped fresh tarragon or 4 teaspoons dried tarragon**
- **Salt**
- **Freshly ground black pepper**
- ¼ **cup unseasoned bread crumbs**
- 2 **tablespoons all-purpose flour**
- 3 **tablespoons vegetable oil**
- **Fresh tarragon sprigs for garnish**

1. Rinse chicken breasts under cold water and pat dry with paper towels. Remove any remaining fat.

2. In bowl, combine egg yolk, mustard, cream, 2 tablespoons chopped tarragon, and salt and pepper to taste; set aside.

3. In another bowl, combine bread crumbs and remaining 2 tablespoons chopped tarragon. Dust chicken breasts with flour.

4. Dip each chicken breast into mustard-egg mixture, letting excess drip back into bowl; coat with herbed bread crumbs.

5. Place coated chicken breasts on platter; cover and let rest in refrigerator at least 30 minutes to absorb flavors and set crumbs.

6. Heat oil in heavy skillet until hot. Fry breasts until golden, 8 minutes per side. Drain on paper towels. Garnish with tarragon sprigs.

Makes 4 servings

Batter-Fried Broccoli

*W*hen deep-frying, it is very important that the oil is the right temperature, around 350°F. If the oil is too hot, the food browns on the outside but does not cook through inside. If it's not hot enough, the batter absorbs too much oil. Test-fry a piece of batter-dipped broccoli until it is crisp and golden brown. Taste it and then adjust the temperature of the oil as necessary. Be sure the broccoli is dry before dipping in batter. Let the excess batter drip off before frying. Use a deep-fry thermometer, if you have one.

What You'll Need

- **2 pounds broccoli**
- **1½ ounces Parmesan cheese**
- **1 bunch fresh parsley**
- **1 cup all-purpose flour**
- **½ cup bread crumbs**
- **3 eggs**
- **½ cup milk**
- **Pinch of salt**
- **4½ to 5 cups vegetable oil**

1. Thoroughly wash broccoli and cut off larger stems. Divide into individual small florets.

2. Cook florets 2 minutes in boiling salted water. Remove with slotted spoon and set aside to dry.

3. Grate Parmesan. Wash parsley; pat dry. Reserve some sprigs for garnish, if desired. Remove stems and finely chop leaves of remaining parsley.

4. Mix flour, bread crumbs, Parmesan, eggs, milk, salt, and chopped parsley. Dip broccoli into batter.

5. Heat oil in heavy pan to 350°F. Test-fry 1 broccoli piece; adjust temperature if necessary. Add broccoli; fry until crisp and brown, about 3 minutes.

6. Drain broccoli on paper towels. Garnish with parsley sprigs or basil (as shown), and serve hot, with dip, if desired.
Makes 4 servings

Turkey Pot Pie

Filling and flavorful, this deep-dish turkey pot pie is an easy and creative way to use up turkey leftovers. The flaky crust, made from frozen puff pastry, crowns a hearty filling of turkey, liver, bacon, herbs, and a splash of sherry. Baked in an ovenproof bowl, it's ready to go straight to the table. Delicious warm or cold, this pot pie is especially convenient made ahead; just reheat and serve with a salad on a busy weekday night. It's also a great take-along to a potluck dinner.

What You'll Need

- 1 package (17¼ ounces) frozen puff pastry
- 2 onions
- 3 tablespoons chopped fresh parsley
- 1 teaspoon lemon thyme
- 1 pound turkey fillet
- 5 ounces turkey livers
- 3½ ounces bacon
- 2 eggs
- Salt and black pepper to taste
- Freshly grated nutmeg
- ¾ cup dry sherry
- 1 egg yolk

1. Preheat oven to 450°F. Let puff-pastry dough thaw. Chop onions, parsley, and lemon thyme very finely.

2. With a sharp knife, cut turkey, turkey livers, and bacon into very small cubes on a cutting board.

3. Combine onions, herbs, and meat in large bowl. Add eggs, salt, pepper, nutmeg, and sherry; mix well. Grease 1-quart soufflé dish or ovenproof bowl.

4. Line prepared dish with 1 puff-pastry sheet. Trim top; save scraps for decorating crust. Spoon in filling.

5. Place puff-pastry sheet over top. Cut off excess dough. Press upper and lower crusts together.

6. Make small hole in top with cookie cutter; crimp edge with fork. Brush with lightly beaten egg yolk; bake 10 minutes. Reduce oven temperature to 350°F; bake 30 to 35 minutes.
Makes 4 servings

Horseradish Sauce with Apples

For centuries, horseradish cream sauce has been the classic accompaniment to roast beef or prime rib. The sauce is easy to prepare and also tastes scrumptious with roast pork, chicken, smoked fish, steamed broccoli, cauliflower, or baked potatoes. If you prefer freshly grated horseradish, buy smooth, light brown roots that are free of spots or sprouts. Peel and grate the root quickly and avoid breathing the fumes or touching your eyes.

What You'll Need

- **2 crisp, tart apples, such as Cortland, Macoun, Pippin, or Gala**
- **3 ounces (about ⅓ cup) prepared white horseradish or 2 to 3 tablespoons freshly grated horseradish**
- **1 tablespoon plus 2 teaspoons whole blanched almonds**
- **½ cup heavy cream**
- **Pinch of salt**
- **Pinch of sugar**
- **2 (8-ounce) sterilized glass jars with tight-fitting lids**

1. Peel, halve, and core apples. With hand grater or food processor fitted with grating disk, coarsely grate apples.

2. Place grated apples in large bowl. Stir in horseradish; toss until evenly combined.

3. In blender or spice grinder, finely grind almonds. Add ground almonds to apple and horseradish mixture.

4. Pour cream into chilled bowl. With electric mixer, beat cream until stiff peaks form.

5. Gently fold whipped cream into horseradish and apple mixture. Season with salt and sugar. Mix thoroughly.

6. Serve sauce immediately. For gifts, fill 2 sterilized jars with sauce and seal. Top jars with pretty cloth square and tie on with raffia and hanging gift tag.
Makes 2 (8-ounce) jars

Classic
Carrot Cake

For this classic cake to achieve a chewy but light texture, the carrots must be grated finely and the egg whites beaten until stiff but not dry. Make sure the bowl and the beaters used for the whites are completely clean and dry. Present the marzipan carrot-topped cake to your hostess in a handsomely decorated reusable container, as a gift within a gift.

What You'll Need

Cake

- **10 ounces carrots, peeled and trimmed**
- **1 lemon**
- **5 eggs, separated**
- **4 tablespoons water**
- **1 teaspoon vanilla extract**
- **1¼ cups granulated sugar**
- **Pinch of salt**
- **1½ cups chopped toasted walnuts**
- **1 teaspoon baking powder**
- **½ cup bread crumbs**
- **2 tablespoons light rum**

Icing and Garnish

- **1⅔ cups confectioners' sugar, sifted**
- **2 tablespoons light rum**
- **2 tablespoons fresh lemon juice**
- **1 marzipan carrot**

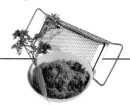

1. Grate carrots. Wash and dry lemon. Grate 1 tablespoon peel and squeeze 2 tablespoons juice. Preheat oven to 325°F. Line 8-inch springform pan with parchment.

2. In large bowl, beat egg yolks, water, vanilla, and sugar. In separate clean bowl, beat egg whites and salt until stiff.

3. Gently fold egg whites into yolk mixture. Add carrots, lemon peel, lemon juice, and remaining cake ingredients; whisk until well blended.

4. Pour batter into prepared pan; smooth top with spatula. Bake 1 hour or until toothpick inserted in center comes out clean. Let cool in pan on wire rack before removing pan side.

5. For icing, combine sifted confectioners' sugar, rum, and lemon juice; stir until blended and smooth.

6. Invert cake onto serving platter; peel off parchment. Spread cake with icing; garnish with marzipan carrot.

Makes 1 (8-inch) cake

Strawberry & Rhubarb Compote

Rhubarb is generally considered to be a fruit, but botanically it is a vegetable. Only the stalks are edible; the leaves must be completely removed because they contain poisonous oxalic acid. Choose crisp, bright stalks with fresh-looking leaves. Since rhubarb is highly perishable, refrigerate it immediately and use within 3 days. Fresh strawberries and fresh rhubarb are readily available in spring, but frozen fruit can be substituted.

1 **pound fresh rhubarb**

½ **cup water**

1 **cup sugar**

½ **pound fresh strawberries**

½ **lemon**

½ **cup red currant jelly**

Whipped cream for garnish

1. Wash, trim, and carefully peel rhubarb stalks. Cut rhubarb into 1-inch pieces.

2. Combine water and sugar in nonreactive pan; heat, stirring constantly, until sugar has dissolved completely.

3. Add rhubarb pieces and stir to coat with syrup. Cover pan and simmer gently for 4 to 5 minutes.

4. Wash, hull, and halve strawberries. Squeeze juice from ½ lemon. Add strawberries and juice to rhubarb.

5. Gently simmer rhubarb and berries for 2 more minutes. Add red currant jelly; stir until well blended.

6. Let compote cool, then transfer to serving bowl. Serve warm or chilled. Garnish individual servings with dollops of whipped cream.

Makes 4 to 6 servings

Ladyfinger Chocolate Cake

Every hostess would love to serve an elegant dessert that is easy to prepare and requires no baking. This mouthwatering chocolate cake may be just the answer. Made with layers of chocolate cream and ladyfingers softened in milk, then piped with whipped cream and garnished with a sprinkling of powdered chocolate, this cake is the perfect conclusion to a formal dinner. Prepare the ladyfinger cake ahead of time, then cover and chill until it is ready to garnish and serve.

What You'll Need

- 1½ cups whole milk, divided
- 3 egg yolks
- 10 tablespoons unsalted butter, softened
- 8 ounces semisweet chocolate, cut into pieces
- 10 ounces purchased ladyfingers
- ½ teaspoon vanilla extract
- 1¼ cups whipped cream
- Powdered chocolate or cocoa powder for garnish

1. Heat 1 cup milk in saucepan over low heat until warm. Whisk in egg yolks and heat until bubbles appear.

2. Beat butter until fluffy; set aside. Melt chocolate in heatproof bowl set over simmering water; stir occasionally.

3. Mix butter and melted chocolate until blended. Add yolk mixture and stir until blended; set aside. Combine remaining ½ cup milk with vanilla.

4. Place ladyfingers in single layer in shallow dish. Pour milk mixture over ladyfingers; let soak until liquid is absorbed.

5. Line 8-inch springform pan with freezer paper. Arrange half of ladyfingers close together in pan. Cover with half of chocolate cream. Repeat layers.

6. Cover; chill 45 minutes or until firm. Invert onto serving platter. Peel off paper; top with whipped cream and powdered chocolate.

Makes 1 (8-inch) cake

Baked Stuffed Apples

For this dessert, use flavorful apples that will hold their shape when baked, such as Baldwin, Cortland, Northern Spy, Jonagold, Ida Red, Rome Beauty, and Winesap. Choose apples that are firm, brightly colored, and free of bruises. Store the apples in a cool, dark place, or refrigerate them in a perforated plastic bag until ready to use. Use an apple corer to remove the cores neatly and enlarge the holes as desired.

What You'll Need

- **4 medium baking apples**
- **4 pieces zwieback or plain cookies of comparable size**
- **2 tablespoons raisins, soaked in rum 30 minutes or until plump**
- **2 tablespoons chopped toasted walnuts**
- **4 tablespoons honey**
- **1 tablespoon lemon juice**
- **3 tablespoons unsalted butter, divided**
- **1 teaspoon anise seeds**
- **Confectioners' sugar for dusting**
- **1 cup whipped cream**

1. Wash apples; pat dry with paper towels. Using apple corer, neatly remove cores and seeds.

2. For filling, crumble zwieback into small bowl. Stir in rum-soaked raisins, walnuts, honey, and lemon juice.

3. Preheat oven to 400°F. Divide filling equally among apples. Melt 1 tablespoon butter. Brush baking apples with melted butter.

4. Place apples in prepared baking dish. Cut remaining 2 tablespoons butter into bits; dot apples with butter.

5. Sprinkle apples with anise seeds. Bake on middle rack of oven 20 to 25 minutes or until soft and golden.

6. Let apples cool slightly; transfer to dessert plates. Dust with confectioners' sugar and serve with whipped cream.
Makes 4 servings

Melon-Lime Party Punch

There is nothing more refreshing on a hot summer day than a tall, ice cold glass of a delicious thirst-quenching beverage. Topped off with a skewer of juicy fresh-fruit tidbits and a slice of lime, this melon-lime drink will be a fun treat for your guests. Use any variety of melon, or experiment by using a combination of melons. Honeydews and cantaloupes impart the sweetest flavor and fruitiest aroma. To make preparation a real breeze, use a blender and an electric ice crusher.

What You'll Need

- 1 honeydew melon
- 1 lime
- 1 to 3 tablespoons clover honey
- About 12 ice cubes
- Assorted summer fruits
- Fresh mint sprigs for garnish

1. Cut melon in half. With spoon, scoop out seeds and fibers; let melon drain into colander set over bowl.

4. Purée fruit mixture until smooth. Add honey; mix until blended. Taste and adjust sweetness, if necessary.

2. Cut melon half into 8 slices. Remove rind and cut up flesh. Add melon and juices from bowl to blender.

5. Wrap ice cubes in kitchen towel; crush with meat mallet or rolling pin, or use electric ice crusher.

3. Slice lime in half; cut 3 thin slices and reserve for garnish. Using citrus juicer, squeeze lime halves. Add lime juice to melon in blender.

6. Divide ice among 3 tall glasses. Fill glasses with melon mixture; stir. Add lime slice, mint sprig, and skewer of fruit for garnish.

Makes 3 (7-ounce) servings

Southern Pecan Pie

*O*nce a specialty found mainly in the Deep South, this luscious pie has achieved countrywide popularity. The flaky butter crust is filled with an ultra-rich mixture of eggs, brown sugar, maple syrup, lemon juice, vanilla bean, melted butter, cornstarch, and chopped pecans and baked until golden. Perfect for a Fourth of July barbecue, this pie can also be served warm with a dollop of whipped cream or a scoop of vanilla ice cream to top off an elegant meal.

What You'll Need

Crust

1¾ cups all-purpose flour

Pinch of salt

7 tablespoons cold butter, cut into pieces

4 to 5 tablespoons ice water

Filling

3 eggs

¼ cup packed light brown sugar

6 tablespoons pure maple syrup

2 teaspoons lemon juice

Seeds from 2 vanilla beans

Pinch of salt

3½ tablespoons unsalted butter, melted and cooled

2 teaspoons cornstarch

2¼ cups coarsely chopped pecans

1. For crust, sift flour into mixing bowl. Add salt and butter; cut in with pastry blender or 2 knives.

2. Add ice water by spoonfuls, mixing until dough holds together. Knead; cover and let rest for 2 hours.

3. For filling, combine eggs, sugar, maple syrup, and lemon juice; whisk until sugar is dissolved. Add vanilla seeds, salt, and butter; whisk until well blended.

4. Whisk in cornstarch. Preheat oven to 425°F. Grease and flour 10-inch springform pan.

5. Roll out pastry; fit into prepared pan. Prick dough with fork; line with foil. Fill with pie weights, uncooked rice, or dried beans. Bake 10 to 15 minutes; remove foil and weights.

6. Reduce oven temperature to 350°F. Fold pecans into filling; pour into partially baked crust. Bake for 30 minutes or until filling is set.

Makes 1 (10-inch) pie

Rice Pudding with Apples

One of the most popular dessert foods, rice pudding is a very basic dish. But it doesn't have to be, as this version proves. If you are transporting the pudding, omit the butter and cinnamon-sugar topping. Just before you are ready to serve the pudding, heat it up, then drizzle with the butter and sprinkle with the cinnamon-sugar. If you are serving the pudding cold, omit the butter drizzle.

What You'll Need

- 2 medium tart apples
- 12 tablespoons (¾ cup) water, divided
- 1 strip orange peel
- 1 cinnamon stick
- 1 quart whole milk
- Pinch of salt
- 1 cup long-grain white rice
- 1 package vanilla pudding mix
- ½ cup plus 2 tablespoons sugar, divided
- 2 egg yolks
- 2 egg whites, stiffly beaten
- 2 teaspoons ground cinnamon
- 2 tablespoons unsalted butter

1. Peel, core, and quarter apples; cut into thin slices. In nonreactive pot, combine apple slices and 6 tablespoons water.

2. Add orange peel and cinnamon stick; bring to a boil. Reduce heat and cook, covered, for 15 minutes.

3. In separate pot, bring milk, salt, and rice to a boil; reduce heat; simmer, covered, for about 20 minutes.

4. Combine pudding mix and remaining 6 tablespoons water; stir until smooth. Stir in ½ cup sugar and egg yolks. Add yolk mixture to rice; bring to a boil.

5. Remove from heat. Fold egg whites into pudding. Alternately layer pudding and apples in serving bowl. Mix cinnamon and remaining 2 tablespoons sugar.

6. Melt butter and drizzle over pudding. Sprinkle evenly with cinnamon-sugar. Serve warm or cold, as desired.

Makes 4 to 6 servings

Peanut Cookies

For the best flavor and texture in these cookies, use unsalted roasted peanuts, available in jars at most supermarkets, and unsalted creamy peanut butter, preferably the freshly ground, preservative-free type sold at health food stores and at many supermarkets. You can also shell your own peanuts: For $\frac{1}{2}$ pound of shelled peanuts, you'll need about $\frac{3}{4}$ pound unshelled. For chocolate peanut butter cookies, add semisweet chocolate chips to the dough with the peanuts.

What You'll Need

- **8 tablespoons (1 stick) unsalted butter, softened**
- **¾ cup creamy peanut butter**
- **1 cup packed light brown sugar**
- **2 eggs**
- **1 teaspoon ground cinnamon**
- **2 cups all-purpose flour**
- **1 rounded teaspoon baking powder**
- **8 ounces unsalted roasted peanuts**

1. Preheat oven to 350°F. Line baking sheet with parchment. In large bowl, with mixer, beat butter, peanut butter, and brown sugar until well blended.

2. Add eggs and cinnamon to peanut butter mixture. Beat until well blended and smooth.

3. Sift flour and baking powder over peanut butter mixture; stir until white streaks disappear. Batter will be stiff.

4. Add peanuts to mixture; knead until evenly distributed.

5. With moist hands, shape dough into equal-size balls; place 3 inches apart on prepared baking sheet.

6. Flatten balls slightly. Bake for 15 to 18 minutes or until cookies are golden brown; cool completely on wire rack.
Makes about 4 dozen cookies

Triple Chocolate Cupcakes

These mouthwatering frosted chocolate cupcakes, ideal for a party, have a hidden secret—they are full of chocolate chips! Serving dessert cupcakes in their own paper wrappers is much easier than slicing a cake and doesn't require any utensils. You can decorate the little cakes in a host of imaginative ways: with clown or animal faces, sugar flowers, initials, hearts, sprinkles, or whipped cream, depending upon the occasion and the age of your guests.

What You'll Need

Cupcakes

- 5 tablespoons butter, softened
- 1 cup packed brown sugar
- 1 tablespoon granulated sugar
- 1 egg
- 1½ teaspoons vanilla extract
- 1 cup whole milk
- 2¼ cups all-purpose flour
- 2 teaspoons baking powder
- Pinch of salt
- 4 teaspoons cocoa powder
- ¼ cup chocolate chips

Frosting and Decoration

- 2 tablespoons butter, softened
- 1 cup confectioners' sugar
- 1 teaspoon vanilla extract
- 3 tablespoons all-purpose flour
- 2 teaspoons cocoa powder
- About 1½ ounces mineral water
- Sugar flowers

1. Preheat oven to 350°F. Line muffin pan cups with paper liners. Blend butter, sugars, and egg. Add vanilla and milk.

2. Sift in flour, baking powder, and salt. Stir in cocoa until smooth. Stir in chocolate chips.

3. Fill muffin cups ⅔ full with batter; bake in center of oven until toothpick inserted in centers comes out almost clean, about 20 minutes. Cool in pans on wire racks 10 minutes; remove from pans. Place on racks to cool completely.

4. For frosting, beat butter, confectioners' sugar, vanilla, flour, cocoa, and 1 ounce mineral water until blended and smooth. Add more mineral water by teaspoonfuls until desired consistency is reached.

5. After cupcakes have cooled, spoon on frosting and spread evenly to cover tops.

6. Arrange cupcakes in their paper liners on plate decorated with paper doily. Decorate tops of cupcakes with sugar flowers.

Makes 20 cupcakes

Grandmother's Apple Cake

One whiff of freshly baked apple cake unlocks many fond childhood memories. Today's hectic pace limits such indulgences, but with thawed, frozen sweet yeast dough, you can produce an excellent facsimile with minimal fuss. For the best flavor and texture, use tart apples, such as Baldwin, Cortland, Granny Smith, Northern Spy, or Winesap. Make sure to overlap the apple slices so that the dough is completely covered.

What You'll Need

- 1 package (16 ounces) frozen sweet yeast dough
- ⅔ cup golden raisins
- 2 tablespoons rum
- Juice of 1 lemon
- 2¼ pounds tart apples
- 4 to 5 tablespoons apple jelly
- 1 tablespoon water

1. Thaw dough as directed on package; let rise. Lightly grease 10-inch springform pan. Line bottom and side of prepared pan with dough.

2. Preheat oven to 400°F. Combine raisins and rum; let soak. Fill large bowl with cold water; add lemon juice.

3. Peel, halve, and core apples; cut into thick slices. Place apple slices in lemon water to prevent discoloration.

4. Drain raisins; reserve rum for glaze. Drain apple slices and pat dry with paper towels.

5. Cover dough completely with apples, overlapping slices; sprinkle with raisins. Bake for 35 minutes or until bubbly.

6. For glaze, heat apple jelly, reserved rum and water until melted and smooth. Brush warm glaze over hot cake. Serve warm.

Makes 1 (10-inch) cake

Bread Pudding with Apples

There are few foods as satisfying as bread pudding, especially when prepared with apples and served with a luscious caramel sauce. You can use any white bread for this tasty pudding. However, if the bread has an extra-crispy crust, trim it before toasting the slices. Tart apples, such as Granny Smith, Jonathan, or Northern Spy, are best for flavor. Placing the pudding in a water bath, or bain-marie, cooks the pudding more gently.

What You'll Need

Bread Pudding

1¼ pounds tart apples

6 large slices white bread (about 8 ounces)

⅓ cup packed light brown sugar

2 teaspoons ground cinnamon

8 tablespoons (1 stick) unsalted butter, cut into small pieces

1 cup warm water

3½ tablespoons honey

Sauce

2 tablespoons unsalted butter

3 tablespoons packed light brown sugar

1 cup heavy cream

2 tablespoons dark rum

1 tablespoon ground cinnamon

1. Peel, quarter, and core apples; cut lengthwise into thin slices. Preheat oven to 350°F.

2. Toast bread; tear into small pieces. Grease medium-sized baking dish. Combine brown sugar and cinnamon.

3. Arrange bread and apples in alternating layers, starting and ending with layer of bread, sprinkling each layer with cinnamon-sugar and dotting with butter pieces. Combine water and honey until smooth.

4. Drizzle honey mixture over pudding. Place baking dish in pan containing enough hot water to come halfway up sides of dish. Bake on middle rack of oven about 45 minutes.

5. For sauce, in heavy pan, melt 2 tablespoons butter over medium heat.

6. Add sugar to pan and cook until golden. Whisk in cream, rum, and cinnamon; bring to a boil. Remove sauce from heat; serve with pudding.

Makes 4 servings

Creamy Vanilla Sauce

Every cook knows the value of a good sauce. This delicious sauce is wonderful over baked apples or even chocolate mousse. Do not discard the vanilla bean after straining the sauce. Rinse it under cold water, pat dry, and store it in an airtight container for future use. Vanilla beans can be used up to 4 times. To make vanilla sugar to use for baking or to sweeten coffee or tea, bury a whole vanilla bean in a container of 1 to 2 cups of granulated sugar. Secure the lid and set aside for about 1 week before using.

What You'll Need

- **8 ounces heavy cream**
- **1 vanilla bean**
- **¼ cup sugar**
- **5 egg yolks**
- **1 to 2 tablespoons whole milk (optional)**

1. Pour cream into nonreactive pan. Slit vanilla bean in half lengthwise; scrape out seeds.

2. Add seeds and half of bean to cream (reserve other half for future use); bring to a boil, stirring constantly.

3. In top of double boiler, whisk sugar and egg yolks until light-colored. Whisking, gradually pour in hot cream.

4. Over simmering, not boiling, water, whisk sauce vigorously, until smooth and thickened.

5. Pour sauce through fine-mesh sieve set over bowl; remove and reserve vanilla bean half. Cover and chill sauce.

6. Just before serving, stir sauce. If sauce is too thick, whisk in whole milk by teaspoonfuls until desired consistency is reached.

Makes 4 servings

A Gingerbread Heart

These hearts are perfect for any celebration. Simply vary the colors and decorations to suit any special occasion or person. To make a pattern, lightly pencil a 7-inch heart on a sheet of cardboard or card stock; neatly cut it out. To pipe glazes on the hearts divide your chosen glazes among some bowls, add a few drops of water to each making sure that it is not runny, and stir to combine. Transfer the glazes to zip-tight plastic bags and seal. Snip 1 corner and use to decorate the hearts.

1. Heat honey, brown sugar, and butter over medium-low heat; stir until sugar is completely dissolved. Transfer to bowl.

2. Add flour, almonds, cocoa, ginger, lemon peel, and egg to bowl. Mix rum and baking soda; add to bowl. Mix until dough is shiny and no longer sticky.

3. Cover dough with clean, dry towel; leave in cool place for at least 3 hours, preferably overnight.

4. Preheat oven to 350°F. Line baking pan with parchment. On floured surface, roll dough to 18×10-inch rectangle. Using 7-inch pattern (see instructions on page 80), cut out 2 hearts.

5. Place hearts on prepared pan; bake 10 minutes. Let cool.

6. Mix confectioners' sugar, egg white and water to desired consistency. Tint glazes as desired; pipe decorations on hearts. Secure flowers, leaves, and dragées with glaze.

Makes 2 large cookies

Sweets & Treats 81

Fresh Garden Baskets

Rustic baskets stenciled with bright vegetable or fruit motifs make great gift boxes for your garden's harvest. All it takes is three inexpensive slat baskets, four colors of paint, and acetate. Before the stencils are applied, the baskets are coated with diluted paint to let the wood grain show through. The country look is completed by outlining the simple motifs in black. After harvest, these multipurpose baskets are useful in the garden and kitchen.

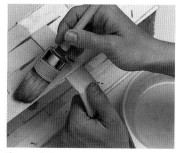

1. In dish, mix blue and white paint to make small amount of light blue. Dilute to thin wash; paint 1 basket. Let dry.

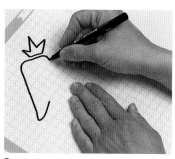

2. With black felt-tipped pen, draw carrot and top (separated by space) onto stencil adhesive. Be sure size of carrot is appropriate to basket size.

3. On cutting mat, use craft knife to carefully cut out carrot and top shape. Remove cutouts.

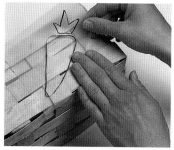

4. Plan layout of motifs. Remove any protective backing from stencil, and smooth stencil into place for first motif.

5. Mix yellow and red paint for orange; mix yellow and blue for green. With lightly loaded brushes, paint carrot and leaves.

6. When paint is dry, remove stencil. Repeat for remaining motifs. When all paint is dry, outline motifs with black pen. Repeat steps for remaining baskets, using other vegetable shapes.

Pretty Painted Birds

No garden would be complete without our feathered friends. Ensure their presence in a friend's garden by cutting some bird forms from plywood and painting them with bright acrylics. Then mount them on brass rods that can be inserted into planters and flowerpots, and the birds will swivel in the wind. The outlines are easy to draw with the help of a compass, French curve, or everyday rounded objects. Browse in a bird book for inspiration!

What You'll Need

French curve, compass, or circular
objects (such as glasses and bowls)

Pencil

Three 6×8-inch pieces plywood,
3⁄8 inch thick each

Coping saw (adult use only)

Medium-grade sandpaper

Acrylic paints: white, blue, red,
yellow, black

Plate

Paintbrushes: large, medium, fine

1⁄8-inch-diameter gimlet (hand drill)
or electric drill and 1⁄8-inch bit

1⁄8-inch-diameter brass rods:
6-inch, 8-inch, 12-inch

Polyurethane (optional)

1. Using French curve, compass, or round shapes and pencil, draw outline of bird on each piece of plywood.

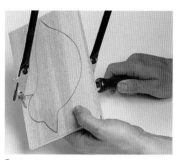

2. Stabilize plywood, and cut along outline of bird with coping saw. (Caution: Saw can be very sharp.) Sand edges with sandpaper.

3. Mix white and blue paints on plate. With larger brush, paint body; let dry. Paint other side.

4. When dry, paint wing, breast, beak, mouth, and eye using fine brush for details. Repeat on other side.

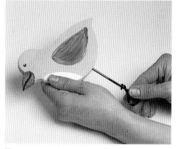

5. Using drill or bit with diameter of brass rod, drill holes in center bottom of birds about 1 1⁄4 to 1 1⁄2 inches deep.

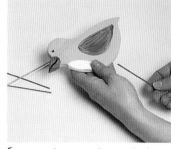

6. Insert brass rods into holes at bottom of birds. If desired, apply 2 coats of polyurethane to protect paint. Insert rod in planter.

Krafty Kitchen Organizer

*K*now someone who
needs a little help in the
kitchen organizing spices,
herbs, and other ingredients?
From this wall-mounted
wooden spoon, three pretty
cones hold whatever
lightweight culinary essentials
you choose. The cones, sewn
from fabrics that complement
any kitchen decor, are
reinforced with easy iron-on
interfacing and decorated with
bright ribbon bows. The cones
hang effortlessly from cup
hooks screwed into the handle
of the spoon.

What You'll Need

Pencil

Ruler

Scissors

½ sheet bond paper (8½×5½ inches)

3 coordinated fabric pieces, each 11×16 inches

1 yard fusible interfacing

Iron

Pins

Sewing machine

Needle and thread

3 small rings

20-inch-wide satin ribbon in each of 3 colors to complement fabrics

1 wooden spoon, about 20 inches long

5 small cup hooks

2 nails or screws

1. To make cone pattern, mark diagonal on paper; cut out. Fold fabric piece in half to measure 8×11 inches.

2. Pin 8½-inch pattern edge to folded fabric edge. Allowing ½ inch along diagonal and 2½ inches excess at top, cut out cone.

3. Using pattern, cut interfacing as in step 2, adding ½-inch side seam allowance but no extra at top. Iron onto back of cutout fabric.

4. Pin right sides together. At raw edge, where 2½-inch excess extends beyond interfacing, cut corner on angle as shown.

5. With ½-inch seam allowance, sew back seam, pivoting at angle and maintaining ½-inch seam allowance. Turn right-side out. Fold flap at top inside cone; press.

6. In middle of back of cone, 2 inches from top, sew on small ring. Make bow; slip-stitch to cone. Make 2 remaining cones in same manner.

7. To attach cones to spoon, position cones evenly along handle and mark center of each cone's ring. Screw cup hooks into handle at these spots. Hang spoon by 2 other cup hooks, which can be attached to screws or nails in wall.

Henny the Egg Holder

A lthough eggs must be stored in the refrigerator, they cook more evenly and achieve greater volume if they are at room temperature. This delightful hen-shaped hanging rack has two shelves with egg-size holes to hold eggs as they warm up prior to use. The simple shape is cut from plywood with a jigsaw and then painted with acrylics. The holes are cut with an electric drill. Any friend will be happy to hang this helpful hen above their kitchen counter!

What You'll Need

- Round object (such as plate or glass) or French curve
- Ruler
- Pencil
- Felt-tipped pen
- 12×12-inch plywood, ⅜ inch thick
- Jigsaw (adult use only)
- Medium-grade sanding block or paper
- Narrow paint roller and paintbrushes
- Acrylic paints: white, blue, orange, black
- 2 wood strips, 8×2×⅜-inch each
- Scrap wood
- Electric drill and 1⅜-inch-diameter Forstner bit
- 4 metal angle brackets and screws
- Screwdriver
- 2 picture hangers
- 2 nails
- Hammer

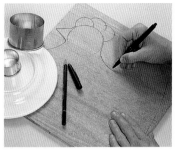

1. Using round object or French curve, draw large hen shape on plywood with pencil. Retrace outline with pen.

2. With jigsaw, cut out hen following outline. (Caution: Saw is very sharp.) With sanding block, sand edges smooth.

3. With roller, paint hen with 2 coats of white paint. Let dry between coats. With brush, paint edges white.

4. Mark holes in wood strips by drawing a line across the center of each. Mark center of the outer holes 1³⁄₁₆ inches from the edges, then mark center of adjacent holes 1⅞ inches from those marks, which leaves ½ inch of wood between them. To prevent chipping, clamp each strip to a piece of scrap wood before cutting the holes.

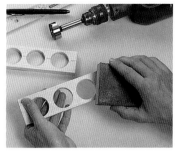

5. With drill, bore holes. Sand strips and holes.

6. Paint strips blue; outline hen and comb with blue. Paint beak orange and eye and mouth black.

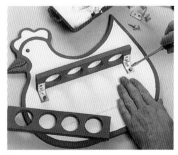

7. Mark placement of strips on hen, with lower strip 3½ inches below top one. Attach brackets to strips, then to hen. Paint brackets. Attach picture hangers to back of hen. Hang on nails in wall.

Piglet Kitchen Blackboard

A kitchen blackboard is a useful tool for communicating messages. Your friend will want to keep this board in a central place so family members can look there for reminders of school events, appointments, shopping lists, and even love notes. This piglet-shaped blackboard fits right into a country kitchen, but you can make a blackboard of any shape to accommodate any decor or preference. You may want to make one for your own kitchen!

1. On cardboard, using compass or round form and French curve, draw pig outline. Cut out pattern.

2. Position pattern on plywood. Trace around outline of pattern to transfer shape to plywood.

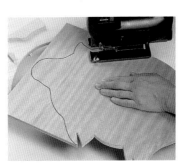

3. On protected work surface, carefully use jigsaw or saber saw to cut shape from plywood.

4. With sanding block, sand top and edge of plywood. Sand in direction of wood grain, not across it.

5. Paint top and edge with 2 coats of chalkboard paint, letting first coat dry before applying second coat.

6. With silver paint marker, draw around outer edge of pig. Add snout, eye, ears, mouth, and tail. Set up in kitchen with chalk and eraser.

Animal Cheese Placards

The variety of cheeses now available is astounding, but this abundance can be confusing at a buffet table. These charming placards let guests know the type of milk—cow's, goat's, or sheep's—from which each cheese was made. With patterns traced from a book or magazine, the signs are easily made from balsa wood. Supported by skewers inserted into the cheese, the tags are both informative and decorative.

What You'll Need

- Soft pencil
- Animal patterns
- Tracing paper
- Black felt-tipped pen
- $3/16 \times 4 \times 20$-inch balsa wood
- Cutting mat
- Craft knife (adult use only)
- 1 tablespoon white acrylic paint, thinned with water
- Paintbrush
- Colored markers
- 3 wooden skewers
- Hot glue gun, glue sticks

1. Using pencil, trace patterns of cow, sheep, and goat onto tracing paper. Redraw with black pen.

2. Place patterns on balsa wood. Using some pressure, draw over design lines with pencil. Remove patterns.

3. On balsa wood, use black felt-tipped pen to fill in indentations made by drawing lines of patterns.

4. On cutting mat, use craft knife to cut out animals, leaving space around pattern. Paint both sides white, letting paint dry before painting other side.

5. When paint is dry, color in animals and backgrounds with colored markers, following black lines. Color both sides.

6. When ink is dry, redraw black outlines. Carefully insert pointed end of skewer into middle of bottom edge of each placard; glue in place if necessary. Insert into cheeses.

Fetching
Tea Towels

Add a whimsical stenciled design to a plain tea towel to turn the ordinary into something special. These black-and-white cows walking along the red border of the white towel are a charming country motif. Red is picked up in the clover, and a spot of yellow for the bell enlivens the whole towel. There are hundreds of stencils from which to choose. What's more, stenciling is easy to do, especially when applied with a foam roller and washable fabric paint. Make a pair for a cheerful gift.

What You'll Need

Tea towels

Acrylic stencil(s)

Tape

Repositionable spray adhesive

Brown paper

Black fabric paint

Paint tray

Foam paint roller

Fabric markers: red, yellow

— Crafting Tips —

Before you paint the towels, wash them to remove any sizing and iron them to eliminate wrinkles. Protect your work surface with brown paper.

1. Determine placement of design on towel. With tape, cover motifs on stencil that will not be painted first.

2. Spray back of stencil with thin, even coat of repositionable adhesive, following manufacturer's instructions.

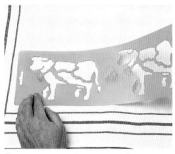

3. Cover work area with paper; spread out and smooth towel. Check placement, and adhere stencil.

4. Pour small amount of desired textile paint into tray and roll it evenly onto foam roller, coating it thoroughly.

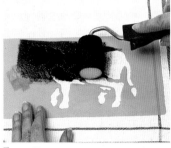

5. Roll paint over areas to be painted in selected color; let dry completely. Remove stencil, wash with water, and dry.

6. Remove tape. Replace stencil, aligning painted motifs. Paint smaller areas with markers; let dry. Heat set paint according to manufacturer's instructions.

Birdseed Ornaments

Truly a gift that keeps on giving, these pretty birdseed ornaments first decorate a Christmas tree and then go outdoors to feed the winter birds. The suet and mixed birdseed that fill the cookie cutters provide healthy sustenance for our feathered friends when other food sources are scarce. A single ornament makes a charming holiday gift for a bird-watcher, or tie several to an evergreen bough along with a bird ornament and a ribbon bow to create a table arrangement.

1. Cut suet into cubes. Place in large pot and heat, stirring constantly, until suet has melted completely.

4. Let cool completely. Wrap cord around each form to hang it upright. Leave excess cord at top for tying to tree.

2. If any pieces of solids surface, skim them out with slotted spoon. Let melted fat cool slightly; stir in birdseed.

5. For table decoration, tie feeders to branches in attractive display.

3. Place cookie cutters on baking sheet. Spoon in almost-solid suet-and-birdseed mixture up to top rim.

6. To complete table decoration, tie ribbon into bow around branch of bough and attach bird ornament.

Makes 6 to 8 ornaments

Punched Metal Container

Punching holes in metal is a decorative technique that was often used in Colonial America to embellish useful objects. Using a nail and hammer, and following a pattern that has been transferred to the surface of a simple galvanized planter, punch holes close together to produce an attractive design. Pretty and practical, this metal container can serve as a desk or kitchen catchall or as a flowerpot. It makes a lovely housewarming gift.

What You'll Need

Fine-tipped dark felt marker

White paper

Masking tape

Colored transfer paper

Galvanized flowerpot or other container

Pencil

Large nail and hammer

Alcohol, paper towel

— Crafting Tip —

Decide whether you want the holes to go completely through the metal (called piercing) or just to indent it (called chasing). Piercing leaves sharp protrusions, which can be smoothed down with a metal file. The size of the holes and how close together they are depends on the diameter of the nail; nails with thinner shanks have sharper points. Choose a nail large enough to hold comfortably, thick enough to be hammered repeatedly without bending, and pointed enough for your design. You could also use an awl.

1. Draw chosen motif; tape to top of colored transfer paper. Position as desired on 1 side of pot.

2. Pressing steadily with pencil, draw over lines of motif to transfer them to pot.

3. Position and transfer motif on other sides of pot, being sure to place motif at same height and position.

4. With fine-tipped marker, make dots ⅛ inch apart to mark nail holes. (Make space between holes closer or farther apart depending on nail size.)

5. With pot on flat surface, hold nail above each dot; rap nail sharply with hammer. Repeat, if necessary.

6. Wipe off transfer paper residue and ink with alcohol-moistened paper towel.

Gracious Greeting Cards

These handmade floral greeting cards are so beautiful they will be kept long after they deliver their written messages. Brilliantly colored paper flowers glued to cards add dimension and a special homemade touch: Tightly crumpled tissue-paper rosebuds shape a heart, crinkled tissue petals form a lush hydrangea cluster, and a wreath of flowers cut from magazines blooms against a bright white background.

What You'll Need

Scissors

Craft glue

For rose heart card:

3½-inch square white corrugated paper

10-inch length green ribbon, ¼ inch wide

6×9-inch green card

Light pink and dark pink tissue paper, about 4×8 inches

Pink glitter paint pen

For wreath card:

24-inch length sheer pink ribbon, 1½ inches wide

6×9-inch white corrugated paper card

2-inch-diameter white cardboard circle

Flower cutouts

For blue hydrangea card:

4-inch-diameter white cardboard half circle

6×9-inch light green card

Blue fine-tipped marker

8-inch square blue tissue paper

Gold glitter paint pen

1. For heart card, cut heart from corrugated paper. Tie ribbon around heart on a diagonal. Glue to card.

2. Cut tissue paper squares; crumple into tight balls. Alternating colors, glue around heart. Dot with glitter paint.

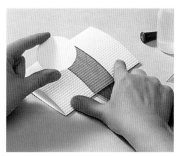

3. For wreath card, fold ribbon in half lengthwise; glue around front middle of corrugated card, leaving ends long at opening. Glue cardboard circle to center front of card.

4. Arrange and glue flower cutouts to circle, overlapping flowers. Tie ribbon into bow at right side of card.

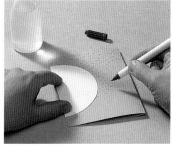

5. For hydrangea card, glue cardboard half circle to bottom of card. Dot all over background with blue marker.

6. Cut tissue squares; crinkle. Glue tissues close together onto half circle. Dot each tissue center with gold glitter.

Spattered-Leaf Gift Decorations

For a fall birthday or anniversary, decorate your special gift with these striking maple leaf trims. Cut from a pattern made from real leaves and spatter-painted in olive green and reddish brown, the lush fall leaves perfectly complement the autumn-colored wrapping paper, the burlap ribbon, the raffia bow, and the gilded seedpod decoration. The leaves can be inserted under the ribbon, used as gift cards, or strung together with gold wire.

1. Place leaves on cardboard. Hold them firmly with 1 hand, and trace. Cut out.

2. Pour paints into bowls. Dip brush into green paint. Holding sieve over cutouts, rub brush against it.

3. Clean and dry brush and sieve. When green paint is dry, repeat spattering with red-brown paint.

4. After paint has dried, fold leaves along lines approximately where veins appear on real leaves.

5. For garland, tie gold wire around stem of leaf. Leave about 2 inches then wrap wire around next leaf stem. Repeat.

6. Wrap gifts, and tie with burlap or paper ribbon. Glue raffia bow, pods, and botanicals to ribbon. Insert leaves under ribbon or arrange garland.

Speckled Enamelware

*O*nce upon a time, speckled white enamelware was found in almost every American kitchen. Now you can re-create that country look on white enamel pieces with a simple paint technique called spattering. A coat of primer seals any cracks and provides a smooth surface for a thin coat of wallpaper adhesive, which holds paint particles that are dispersed by rapping a paintbrush against a hard surface. Varnish protects the finish.

What You'll Need

- **White oil primer**
- **Small mixing bowls**
- **Paintbrush**
- **Enamel bowl**
- **Liquid dishwashing soap**
- **Clean rag**
- **Wallpaper adhesive or wheat paste**
- **Blue oil paint**
- **Paint thinner**
- **Sharpening steel or other hard object**
- **Clear spray varnish**

1. Pour primer into small bowl; stir. Apply thin coat to outside and inside of clean, dry enamel bowl. Let dry.

2. Put small amount of dishwashing liquid on rag, and wipe entire bowl with it to remove dust and impurities.

3. Dilute wallpaper paste until very thin. Brush evenly over outside and inside of bowl. Let dry.

4. Dilute blue oil paint to creamy consistency. Dip brush into paint, then hit it against steel, aiming bristles at bowl.

5. Repeat to spatter entire bowl, inside and outside. Wipe paint off rim of bowl with clean rag.

6. Let bowl dry overnight. Spray with clear varnish. To clean bowl, wipe with damp cloth; do not immerse in water.

Appealing Découpaged Tray

A plain wooden tray is transformed into a handsome serving accessory with découpaged fruit motifs and paint antiquing. The tray needn't be new; découpage is perfect for revitalizing used objects. Use sheets printed specifically for découpage, or cut up wrapping paper, seed packages—even copies of paintings or photographs. Arrange the motifs attractively, distributing them evenly over the space by overlapping them in a montage or repeating them around a border.

What You'll Need

Wooden tray

Acrylic primer (optional)

Acrylic paints: yellow, light brown

Flat paintbrushes

Fine-grade sandpaper or sanding block

Tack cloth

Paper motifs

Small, sharp, pointed scissors

Découpage medium

Clear-drying, water-based polyurethane varnish

Clean, lint-free rags

1. If desired, prime tray. Let dry. Paint entire tray yellow. Let dry. Lightly sand, and use a tack cloth to remove dust. Apply second coat of paint. Let dry.

2. Roughly cut out motifs to be attached, then carefully and precisely cut them out with sharp scissors.

3. Arrange motifs on tray as desired. Apply découpage medium to back of motifs. Press in place, smoothing out wrinkles. Let dry.

4. With brush, apply a smooth, even coat of varnish, working in 1 direction and overlapping strokes slightly.

5. Let dry. Sand gently, and use tack cloth. With lightly loaded rag, rub brown paint across tray. Wipe off excess; let dry.

6. Varnish tray again, and let dry. Sand again, and use tack cloth. Repeat varnishing, drying, sanding, and tacking 3 or 4 more times, ending with varnish. Let dry.

Dazzling Stenciled Tile

A stenciled ceramic tile trivet is decorative and a practical way to protect surfaces from damage. Stencils come in every conceivable design, from country motifs to modern geometrics, and paints specially made for porcelain, ceramic, or glass can be mixed to any desired hue. Once heat-set, the paint becomes washable and durable. These would even make beautiful decorations for a dressing table—make one to match a friend's bedroom decor!

What You'll Need

- **Light-colored glazed tile: clean, dry, grease-free**
- **Stencil (craft stores offer a variety of motifs)**
- **Water-soluble felt-tipped pen**
- **Ruler**
- **Masking tape**
- **Stencil brush**
- **Glass and tile paints**
- **Hot glue gun, glue sticks**
- **Foam or cork circles**

— Crafting Tip —

You can stencil any kind of ceramic kitchenware. Care must be taken to keep a stencil flush against a rounded surface to prevent paint seepage. To flatten out the stencil, slit it vertically and/or use a repositionable spray adhesive rather than tape. When painting 2 distinct colors, cover the cutout area not to be painted with masking tape.

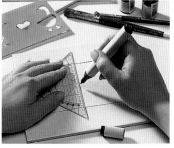

1. Determine placement of motifs. On tile, mark top and bottom of stencil, center of tile, and any other alignment points.

2. On stencil, draw lines at center and other alignment points. Here, a line ¼ inch from beak places goose properly.

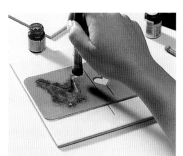

3. Aligning placement lines, tape stencil in place for first motif; paint goose. When completely dry, shift stencil; paint heart.

4. When dry, remove and clean stencil. Flip stencil face down, align, and paint mirror-image on other side of heart.

5. Mark diagonals with pen. In each corner of tile, paint a heart, with point of heart placed on diagonal.

6. When dry, wipe away pen marks, then bake following paint manufacturer's instructions. Turn tile over, and hot glue foam circles to corners.

Natural Gift Wrappings

The recipient of this package won't know whether to open it or display it as a fall centerpiece. Plain brown wrapping paper is transformed with the most natural of materials: dried apple and orange slices, cinnamon sticks, star anise, and raffia. The delicate designs of dried fruit add an imaginative touch to plain paper, not to mention a rich aroma to a room. You may have to remind your friend that there is something just as wondeful inside this pretty package, too!

What You'll Need

Bowl

Large spoon

1 each: lemon, apple, orange

1 teaspoon salt

Paper towels

Jelly-roll pan

Brown wrapping paper

Raffia

3 cinnamon sticks

4 to 5 star anise

Craft glue

— *Crafting Tips* —

Be imaginative when you consider natural materials as decorations. Pinecones, moss, seedpods, flowers, and leaves or bits of bark can all be glued onto a package—and they're free for the taking. Add an attractive bow made from 3 strands of raffia. Tie in some cinnamon sticks, and lace raffia tails through the dried orange slices.

1. Squeeze juice from lemon. In bowl, mix lemon juice and 1 teaspoon salt until salt is entirely dissolved.

2. Cut apple and orange into thin slices.

3. Immerse apple and orange slices in lemon-salt mixture and turn several times, coating completely.

4. Pat slices dry with paper towels. Place in jelly-roll pan; dry in oven at lowest setting for 2 to 3 hours or overnight.

5. Wrap gift in paper; tie lengthwise and widthwise with a triple strand of raffia. Secure cinnamon sticks in knot.

6. Arrange fruit slices and star anise on package. Glue them to paper; let dry completely. Make tag, if desired.

Country Welcome Sign

A move to a new home is a special occasion. Help the new residents welcome their visitors with a charming basket-shaped sign for the front door. Cut from soft spruce with a fret saw, then painted with acrylics in the colors of your choice, the sign is embellished with a row of perky bright-pink tulips. A fine-tipped paint marker makes the lettering and detailing easy. Cover the curved wire hanger with ivy or seasonal flowers, if you like.

What You'll Need

Graph paper

Pencil

Ruler

Scissors

Clamp

⅞×7½×10¼-inch piece spruce or plywood

Fret saw

Drill with small-diameter bit

Medium-grit sandpaper

Acrylic paints: dark blue, ocher, pink, olive green

Paintbrushes

Black paint marker with fine point

Clear acrylic sealer

1 yard silver wire, 18 gauge

Wire cutters

Pliers

Silk ivy vines

1. Cut a sheet of graph paper to 7½×10¼ inches. Fold it in half, aligning short edges, and use the boxes as guides to round the bottom corners. Open the paper and draw a centered rectangle (the boxes make the centering simple) 2¾×6¼ inches wide. Cut out the rectangle to make a stencil.

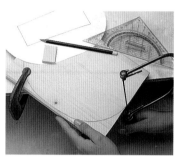

2. Transfer 2 rounded corners onto wood. Clamp wood to work surface; cut with fret saw.

3. About ⅜ inch from edges, drill small holes in top corners. Smooth edges of sign with sandpaper.

4. Paint sign dark blue. Let dry. Lay graph-paper stencil over dried paint. Paint center rectangle ocher. Let dry.

5. Above ocher rectangle, paint a row of pink tulips and olive green leaves.

6. With black paint marker, draw stems, letters, and border design. Also, outline rectangle, tulips, and leaves.

7. Coat with clear sealer. Let dry. Bend wire into kinks (or use shorter length of unkinked wire). Insert ends into holes and close loops with pliers. Twist ivy vines around hanger. Let some ivy trail down sides of sign.

Rolled Beeswax Candles

Beeswax candles are not only handsome, but they are also naturally and deliciously fragrant. The intricate-looking spiraled taper and thick, sawtoothed pillar candle are made by rolling beeswax sheets. This is the simplest of all candlemaking techniques. Beeswax is perhaps loveliest in its natural amber color, but it is also available in white and a rainbow of colors. These creations make a thoughtful gift at the holidays or anytime.

What You'll Need

4 to 5 sheets of beeswax in desired sizes and colors

Ruler

Craft knife

Wicks: square braid in size to fit diameter of candle

Scissors

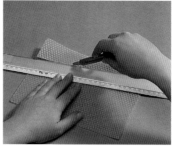

1. For taper, angle ruler lengthwise across wax from 1¹⁄₂ inch down from left corner to top right corner. Trim excess.

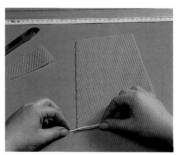

2. Place wick along longer side edge of beeswax, and press it gently into wax. Carefully roll wax evenly over wick.

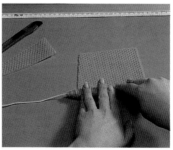

3. Pressing evenly with both hands, roll up beeswax. Keep bottom edge of candle even, creating spiral on top.

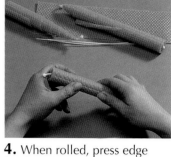

4. When rolled, press edge firmly into candle with fingers. Cut off excess wick at bottom and trim to ¹⁄₄ inch at top.

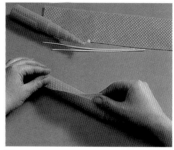

5. If desired, flare edge out slightly to create a decorative flap. Be sure final wrap is securely attached.

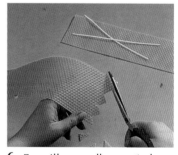

6. For pillar candle, cut 1 short edge of sheet into sawtooth with scissors. Place wick along opposite edge, and roll candle, ending with sawtooth on outside.

Scented Sleep Pillow

*T*here is more to this romantic ruffled pillow than meets the eye. It is filled with a blend of soothing aromatic herbs and essential oil that practically guarantee relaxation and sleep. The sewing techniques are easy, and the dried herbs and essential oil are readily available. By day, it's a beautiful decorative element; by night, it's a comforting presence to ease you into sweet dreams. Use a masculine fabric and eliminate the ruffle to make a thoughtful gift for a man.

What You'll Need

- 24×36-inch cotton fabric
- Scissors
- Sewing machine
- Pins
- Iron
- 2 feet cotton lace, ¾ inch wide
- 5 feet satin ribbon, ⅜ inch wide
- 10-inch pillow form
- Small bowl
- 2 cups dried hops flowers
- ½ cup each dried mint leaves and dried mallow leaves
- 2 ounces dried violet root
- 2 teaspoons cardamom seeds
- 10 drops peppermint essential oil
- Needle and thread

1. Cut cotton fabric into two 11¼-inch squares for the pillow front and back. Also cut two 36×5-inch strips for the ruffle.

2. (Unless otherwise noted, all seam allowances are ⅝ inch.) Place a short end of each strip right sides together. Sew across this short edge to make 1 long strip. Press seam open. To prepare ruffle, fold strip in half widthwise, wrong-sides together, and press.

3. On pillow front, lay strips of lace on equally spaced diagonal lines. Pin in place, and sew along both edges.

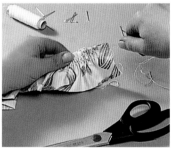

4. Near open edge of ruffle, sew 2 parallel rows of long stitches. Pull threads to make 40-inch gathered ruffle.

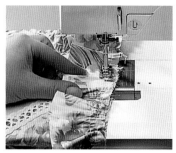

5. Align raw edge of ruffle with edge of pillow front, right-sides together. Pin in place, and sew.

6. Lay pillow front and back with right sides together, and pin in place. Sew together, leaving a 6-inch opening.

7. Turn right side out. Leaving a 10-inch tail, start at corner and sew ribbon to base of ruffle. At end, tie ribbon into bow. Insert pillow form.

8. Assemble herbs and seeds in a bowl, and sprinkle them with peppermint oil. Through opening, fill pillow with herbs. By hand, slipstitch opening closed.

Pleasing Place Mats

Stencil solid-colored place mats with seasonal motifs for an easy, inexpensive, and thoughtful hostess or house-warming gift. These pretty stenciled tulips bring spring to the table. Leaves or vegetables in autumnal colors are perfect for a harvest motif, while holly and snowflakes can adorn the table right through winter. Decorate the whole mat or just the edges—you can even make them match your friend's kitchen decor!

What You'll Need

- **Cardboard or other stencil material**
- **Pencil or felt-tipped pen**
- **Cutting mat**
- **Craft knife (adult use only)**
- **Masking tape**
- **Place mats, washed, dried, and ironed**
- **Stencil brushes: medium, large**
- **Fabric paints: green, red, yellow**
- **Iron**

— *Crafting Tips* —

If you can't use a separate brush for each paint color, wash the brush thoroughly and let it dry before changing colors. To avoid seepage under the stencil, hold your lightly loaded brush perpendicular to the surface and work in from the edges. Build up color gradually, using a circular motion to work the paint into the fibers. Use tape to mask a different-color cutout area that is close to an area you are painting. Try hand-painting details, if you like.

1. Draw tulips on stencil material (or transfer traced motif with graphite paper). Tape tracing to cutting mat. To make repeat design, cut 2 stencils side by side.

2. Using craft knife, carefully cut out motifs. Tape stencil to place mat.

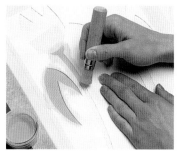

3. Load medium brush lightly with green paint. Hold stencil down, and lightly pounce brush up and down on stem to paint.

4. With larger brush, apply red paint diagonally from top to bottom of tulip. Paint should be heavier in some areas and lighter in others.

5. Fill in top and bottom of tulip with yellow, painting some areas more heavily, softly overlapping and blending with red in others.

6. Let paint dry; remove stencil. If repeating design, reposition stencil and continue. Let dry. Heat-set following paint manufacturer's instructions.

Gift Box for a Gardener

Nothing brightens dark winter days more than thoughts of spring. In the dead of winter, any gardener would be delighted with a special multipurpose gift box filled with flower bulbs, colored stakes, seeds, and a fresh batch of starting pots. Painted in exterior paint so it can do garden duty in any weather, the box itself can hold whatever assortment you choose. Festooned with a garland of boxwood, this enchanting gift is both pretty and practical.

— Crafting Tips —

Wrapped in a burlap sack, bulbs can be kept in a cool, dark place until they are planted in the spring.

1. Paint wooden box on inside, outside, and handle with green paint. If needed, apply second coat. Let dry completely.

2. Paint wooden stakes different colors, letting each side dry before turning and painting other side. Let dry.

3. Place tulip bulbs in center of burlap square. Gather edges; tie closed with woven ribbon.

4. Cut picture of tulip from bulb package or catalog. Punch hole in top. Hang from sack with decorative cord.

5. Cut piece of twine to fit around box. Lay boxwood along twine; secure with gold wire. Hot glue garland to box.

6. Hang miniature flowerpots, evenly spaced, from garland with decorative cord. Arrange bulbs, stakes, flowerpots, seeds, and other items in box.

Leaf-Stenciled Flowerpots

Houseplants make striking decorating accessories, especially in brightly painted terra-cotta pots. Leaf designs are particularly appropriate for flowerpots and are easy to paint using custom-cut stencils. Some simple motifs to consider include leaves, shells, flowers, animals, vegetables, or choose a design that fits a friend's decor. Coordinate the colors and stencil patterns for a pair of pots or make each individual pot unique.

What You'll Need

- **2 terra-cotta flowerpots, 6 inches in diameter each**
- **Acrylic paints: orange, yellow, green**
- **Paintbrushes**
- **Masking tape**
- **Leaf templates**
- **Pencil**
- **Heavy paper**
- **Scissors**
- **Spray varnish or polyurethane**

1. Paint half of 1 flowerpot orange; create scalloped vertical edges. Let dry. Paint other half yellow, matching edges.

2. Paint second flowerpot yellow. Let dry. Apply masking tape below rim to protect painted pot. Paint rim orange.

3. To make stencils, lay leaf templates on heavy paper and draw around them. Carefully cut away insides of shapes.

4. When paint is completely dry, tape stencils onto pots. Tape firmly against curved surface to prevent seepage.

5. Stencil leaves in colors that contrast with background. Use lightly loaded brush, and paint inward from cut edges.

6. When paint is dry, remove stencils. Spray inside and outside of pots with clear varnish to seal and protect.

Antiqued Hatboxes

These hatboxes look as if they came out of great-grandmother's closet. Actually, they are inexpensive bandboxes that have been covered with vintage-looking wallpaper and then "aged" with a crackling medium and ordinary oil paint. Depending upon the box sizes, you might be able to use wallpaper borders or remnants. The trio makes both an attractive display and a great gift, and they can be used for storage if you can't part with them!

What You'll Need

- **Round chipboard or cardboard box with lid**
- **Wallpaper in 2 patterns**
- **Scissors**
- **Ruler**
- **Wallpaper adhesive or craft glue**
- **Crackle medium**
- **Paintbrush**
- **Brown oil paint**
- **Small plate**
- **Clean rag**
- **Paper towels**
- **Matte spray varnish**

1. To cover the hatbox, cut 3 pieces of wallpaper. For around box bottom, cut a piece equal to the circumference + 1½ inches. For the rim of the lid, cut a piece equal to the circumference + 1 inch × the height of the rim + 1½ inches. For the top of the lid, cut a circle exactly the size of the lid top.

2. To cover box bottom, align the paper strip along box's bottom edge. Slit the 1½-inch extension at the top every 1 inch, and glue it neatly to the inside of the box. For the lid, center the rim on the wallpaper strip, then clip and glue the bottom ¾ inch to the inside of the rim and the top ¾ inch over the top of the lid. Glue circle to top of lid.

3. Apply crackle medium to box lid following manufac-turer's instructions. As medium dries, cracks will develop. Let dry.

4. Apply crackle medium to box bottom. Let dry.

5. Pour brown oil paint onto plate. Using clean rag, rub paint evenly over surface of box into cracks.

6. Remove excess paint carefully with paper towel, checking for even coverage and coloring.

7. In well-ventilated place, hold can 12 inches from surface and spray even coat of varnish onto box top and bottom. Let dry completely.

Charming Country Lantern

This charming country luminary exemplifies crafting at its best. What looks like milky glass is sturdy translucent paper, and what appears to be a wrought-iron frame is cleverly cut construction paper. The warm glow from a candle illuminates the hearts and barnyard animals that were drawn using cookie cutters. Any kind of paper works, from Japanese rice paper to white paper bags. For safety's sake, use a votive candle in a clear glass holder.

Heavy black construction paper:
1½×20½-inch strip plus sheets for
shapes

Ruler

Pencil

Scissors

Craft knife (adult use only)

Craft glue

8×20½-inch translucent white paper

2- to 3-inch cookie cutters or
stencils: heart, rabbit, duck,
rooster

8-inch square coaster

Votive candle and holder

1. Fold black paper strip ½ inch from short edge, then 3 times every 5 inches. For grass, cut triangular fringe ¾-inch deep on 1 side.

2. Cut 40 fence pickets ¼×2½ inches. (Some fence posts can be a bit longer or shorter.) Cut 4 cross bars ¼×5 inches.

3. Glue fence pickets to grass about ¼ inch apart. Glue black strip closed, adhering ½-inch fold-over edge.

4. Fold white paper ½ inch from long edge, then 3 times every 5 inches. Glue closed, adhering ½-inch fold-over edge.

5. Glue bottom of lantern inside black strip. Glue a cross bar to top of fence pieces on each side.

6. Using cookie cutters, draw animals on black construction paper. Cut out, and glue to lantern.

7. For the corner posts, cut 4 construction paper strips 12 inches long and ½ inch wide; score and fold them in half lengthwise.

8. Cut down the center of the corner posts 4 inches from tops, and curl ends. Glue posts to corners of lantern. Place lantern on coaster; insert candle. Never leave a lit candle unattended.

Gourd Candle Holders

Ornamental gourds come in an amazing variety of shapes, sizes, colors, and textures, making them a natural choice for autumn decorating. Here, gourds are given a new purpose as miniature candle holders. Six gourds are hollowed out, fitted with tea lights, and, if the rinds permit, punched with cookie cutters to create a pretty carved lantern. The little luminaries are then grouped on a tray amid fresh moss and trailing ivy, making a centerpiece that will warm and beautify a harvest table.

What You'll Need

6 tea lights

6 ornamental gourds

Felt-tipped pen

Heavy, sharp serrated knife

Sharp paring knife

Melon baller or spoon

Cookie cutters

Tray

Fresh sheet moss

Ivy vines, real or silk

1. To calculate dimension of holder, place tea light on top of gourd. Outline rim with felt-tipped pen.

2. With serrated knife, cut top off of gourd, making circumference slightly larger than that of tea light. Even out rough edges with paring knife.

3. Using melon baller or spoon, hollow out gourd so that tea light will fit comfortably inside.

4. For carved gourds, leave shell ½ inch thick. With cookie cutter, punch out motifs.

5. Line tray with moss. Arrange candle holders. Include cut-off tops and motifs in display, if you wish.

6. Place tea lights inside gourds. Wind trailing ivy attractively around and among gourds. Never leave lit candles unattended.

Planted
Flower
Wreath

This floral arrangement is different from most wreaths and centerpieces. Instead of short-lived cut flowers or nostalgic dried flowers, these pretty kalanchoe plants are actually growing in soil in a cardboard wreath base. The bright little red flowers and large glossy green leaves will remain lush for a long time. For added charm, the wreath is decorated with miniature clay ornaments, moss, and a rustic circle of clematis vines.

What You'll Need

Trowel

Potting soil

Concave cardboard wreath form, 10 inches in diameter

5 small kalanchoe plants

Sphagnum moss

7 small clay ornaments

7 green floral stem wires

Wire cutters

Clematis or other flexible vines

Pruning shears

— *Crafting Tips* —

The wreath base shown is a concave circle made of pressed cardboard. If you can't find this type of form at a floral supply store, you can line a concave wire frame with plastic sheeting to hold the soil. With either type, protect your table by placing the wreath on a plate. Kalanchoe and other succulents are well suited for this wreath because they require less watering than other flowering plants. Remove flowers as they wilt, and water only when soil has dried out.

1. With trowel, fill cavity of wreath form almost to rim with potting soil, compressing it lightly.

2. Embed plants around wreath, spacing evenly. Fill in around plants with soil, seating them securely.

3. Press soil down evenly. Divide moss. Place clumps between plants to hide soil; press moss down.

4. For each ornament, slip wire through hole or handles. Bend wire until ends meet, and twist to secure.

5. Distribute ornaments evenly around wreath by inserting ends of wires snugly into moss and soil. You may need to trim wire ends.

6. Wind vines around wreath, clipping as necessary. Weave ends together to hold in place. Keep wreath in a cool, sunny spot, and water as needed.

Pinecone Christmas Tree

Prepare your home for the holidays with a festive tabletop tree made from a flowerpot and a foam cone into which a seasonal array of pinecones, evergreen sprigs, and ribbon bows are inserted. The foam base is concealed by a cuff of longer greenery, and the green felt-covered pot is encircled by wire-edged red ribbon that echoes the warm red of the bows. For a bit of sparkle, rustic pinecones are gilded with gold paint. This durable decoration is sure to lift your holiday spirits.

Terra-cotta flowerpot, about 5½ inches in diameter

Dark green felt, 20 inches square

1½ yards wire-edged red ribbon, 1½ to 2 inches wide

12-inch foam cone

Sprigs of greenery

Hot glue gun, glue sticks

40 to 60 pinecones

Floral pins

3 yards red satin ribbon, ⅜ inch wide

Scissors

Medium-weight floral stem wire

Wire cutters

Gold paint

Fine paintbrush

— Crafting Tips —

Use any kind of locally available evergreen for this tree. Cypress, spruce, pine, cedar, and fir are all attractive, long-lasting, and fragrant. Use longer sprigs to encircle the bottom of the foam, just above the flowerpot rim, to cover the line where the foam meets the felt.

1. Place pot in center of felt. Wrap felt up and over rim of pot. Tie wire-edged ribbon around pot and into a bow.

2. Insert wide end of foam cone into pot. Insert 3½-inch-long sprigs of greenery around bottom of cone. If needed, secure sprigs to cone with glue.

3. Starting at bottom, hot glue pinecones to foam. Glue larger cones to bottom and smaller ones to top.

4. Attach sprigs to floral pins, and insert sprigs to fill in spaces between pinecones.

5. Cut ribbon into 6-inch lengths, and tie into bows. Twist floral wires around centers of bows, and insert bows between evergreens and cones.

6. Brush pinecones and lower cuff of greenery with light coating of gold paint.

A Tangle of Tulip

Let tulips explode into a wild exhibit of exuberant color in any wide-mouthed container. The secret to these seemingly untamed tulips is an ivy wreath that sits atop the vase. Stems of ivy crisscrossed inside give the flowers extra support and clumps of moss fill in the gaps and obscure the underpinnings. The longer the tulips are kept fresh by daily watering, the more likely their cuplike flower heads and long, thick stems will bend and twist to form interesting shapes.

— Crafting Tips —

Weaving an ivy wreath to hold flowers is a simple and effective idea. Make the wreath to fit the container, so you can use anything that appeals to you and holds water. (If it doesn't hold water, insert a liner.)

Tulips will stay fresh longer if only one-third of their stems are immersed in water. Before inserting them, remove any leaves from the lower third and cut the bottoms on an angle. Water daily.

1. Removing leaves as necessary, weave 2 to 3 ivy stems into a wreath that is the same size as floral container rim. Tie with raffia.

2. Weave in ivy stems (reserving 4), working in same direction. Crisscross and attach 4 ivy stems to bottom of wreath with stem wire. This framework will support flowers.

3. Wrap clumps of moss with spooled floral wire. Attach stem floral wire as "stems" for insertion.

4. Remove leaves from bottom third of tulip stems. Cut stem ends on an angle to increase water absorption.

5. Insert tulips through wreath into vase at cross angles.

6. Place clumps of moss between flowers. Insert more tulips in center of wreath, which will be supported by ivy framework.

Colorful Summer Garland

T his rose, sweet William, and hydrangea garland is so brilliant and vibrant it can be used to mark the seat of honor at a summer garden party, to adorn a curving centerpiece on the tabletop, or to decorate the railing leading to your home. Not only is the garland beautiful and versatile, it is also easy to make. What's more, it is economical. It uses everyday popular varieties of flowers and foliage that you may already have growing in your garden or yard.

What You'll Need

- 20-inch length of sisal or other thick rope
- Satin ribbons: red, light blue, dark blue, yellow
- Scissors
- Green spooled floral wire
- Boxwood
- Red and pink sweet William, 20 of each color
- Red and pink roses, 15 of each color
- 5 blue hydrangeas

1. Tie a piece of ribbon to rope to mark its center. Work from 1 end to center, then from other end to center.

2. Leaving tail of wire with which to hang garland, wrap floral wire around 1 end of rope to attach it.

3. Wire on some boxwood, with stems pointing toward center. Wire a few flowers over boxwood. Continue adding boxwood and flowers.

4. As you approach center of rope, widen garland by using larger clusters of flowers and flowers with longer stems. Save most hydrangeas for center of swag.

5. After completing first half, start from opposite end of rope and repeat steps 2, 3, and 4.

6. Tie lengths of ribbons decoratively to ends of garland.

Trailing Ivy Designs

vy, an ever-popular houseplant, can be fashioned into an attractive potted ornament by training it into a topiary—a simple process when you know how. Just bend wire into any shape you like to make a climbing frame, and then weave the tendrils onto it. The upkeep is easy, and the topiaries just get prettier as they grow to fill out the shape. A heart, always inviting, is a graceful, easy form for the ivy to assume. A sphere, made from two intersecting circles, makes an enticing three-dimensional arrangement.

What You'll Need

Paper

Pencil

Scissors

Galvanized wire

Wire cutters

Terra-cotta flowerpots, trowel

General-purpose potting soil

Ivy plants with long tendrils

String

— Crafting Tips —

Use sturdy but bendable 18-gauge wire for the wreath form. It should be galvanized so it won't rust. Wind the long ivy tendrils around the wire, being careful not to crush the shoots and leaves; you want them to continue to grow. Once the topiary is established, you'll be able to weave tendrils through previously wound ivy without having to tie them. Tuck new growth in and around form, and trim as necessary to keep the shape. When the frame is covered, cut back the longer branches to encourage growth.

1. To make heart, fold paper in half. Beginning at crease, draw half of heart. Cut along outline. Unfold, and smooth out.

2. Leaving a 4-inch tail, begin shaping wire at bottom of heart, continuing around pattern. Leaving another 4-inch tail, cut wire.

3. Plant ivy in terra-cotta pot; press soil down. Insert ends of wire heart into soil. Press soil down to secure wire.

4. Wind 2 or 3 long branches of ivy around heart frame, and fasten loosely with string. Don't crush leaves or stems.

5. Twine remaining tendrils carefully around heart frame, tying with string as necessary to maintain shape.

6. To form sphere, cross 2 wire circles at right angles; fasten top and bottom. Plant ivy and wind around both wires.

Wildflower Bouquet

Although it looks like just an armful of flowers and foliage randomly gathered from a country meadow, this free-form bouquet requires a bit of planning. Tall stems of unpretentious blooms are positioned in a classically proportioned arrangement that suits the ceramic pitcher holding it. Gather your own assortment of flowers on a nature walk or purchase them at a farmer's market. Display this kaleidoscope of colors and textures where it can be fully appreciated.

What You'll Need

Various fresh wildflowers, foliage, herbs, and grasses: yarrow, cornflowers, daisies, buttercups, delphiniums, chervil, chamomile, poppies, goldenrod, and Queen Anne's lace

Raffia

Sharp knife or garden shears

Simple ceramic vase or pitcher

— *Crafting Tips* —

Enjoy gathering flowers, but keep courtesy and conservation in mind: Obtain permission from landowners, don't pick endangered species, and don't pick all you see of one botanical. Cut the stems with a sharp knife, leaving the roots intact. When you get home, stand the flowers in water.

1. Remove leaves from lower ²/₃ of stems, which will be immersed in water. Sort materials according to type.

2. Select 3 tall stems for top; hold in 1 hand. Place fourth stem diagonally across these stems from left.

3. Rotating bouquet in hand, continue adding stems diagonally from left, creating spiral of stems.

4. Examine bouquet from all angles. If necessary for symmetry, add flowers around bouquet.

5. When bouquet is of desired size, wrap stems tightly several times with raffia; knot securely.

6. With knife or garden shears, cut stems on slant to same length. Place in water-filled vase. Change water and recut stems frequently to increase longevity.

Festively Fragrant Pinecones

wo large pinecones become the focal point of a tasteful winter arrangement. Decorative wire, ivy, and pearls embellish the naturally intricate and understated beauty of the cones, making them perfectly suited for the holiday festivities. Touched with aromatic oil, they are even more appealing to the senses. A bow of plaid wire-edged ribbon adds color and dimension to the piece.

What You'll Need

Large plate

Moss

2 silk ivy vines

Hot glue gun, glue sticks

Gold beading wire

50 to 60 small pearls

Decorative gold wire, very thin

2 large pinecones

80 to 100 large pearls

Tweezers

Wire-edged ribbon bow

Fragrance oil

— *Crafting Tips* —

Use pinecones you gathered yourself on a late-fall walk in the woods or purchase them at a flower shop. If a pinecone is still closed, place it on a cookie sheet in a 200°F oven for a few minutes to coax it open so it looks larger and more decorative. If you prefer, use several small cones for the arrangement.

1. Cover plate with fresh or dried moss, leaving wide rim around outer edge of plate bare.

2. Drape ivy around outer rim of plate. If necessary, hot glue in place.

3. Tie knot in beading wire; thread on a small pearl. Knot to secure. Continue adding pearls and knotting wire until you have length you need to wrap around edge of plate a few times. Set aside.

4. Wrap decorative gold wire around and across a pinecone in an attractive pattern. Twist ends together to secure.

5. Hot glue large pearls to second pinecone, holding pearls with tweezers to protect fingers.

6. Wind wired pearls through ivy on plate. Arrange pinecones on moss and place bow. Add fragrance oil to pinecones, if desired.

Peonies in a Country Basket

The rose may be considered the queen of flowers, but the peony reigns in many country gardens. Known as the flower of radiance, the peony is one of the loveliest flowers to grow and display. They can be quite large, so most arrangements with peonies are dramatic. Here, a simple basket shows off the lush blossoms while dainty astilbes and delicate bells of Ireland complement the fragrant peonies.

What You'll Need

- Wide decorative ribbon
- Woven basket with handle
- Nylon thread and needle
- Block floral foam
- Knife
- Bowl to fit inside basket
- 8 to 12 pink peonies with leaves
- 6 to 10 wine red astilbes with leaves
- 3 to 7 light green bells of Ireland
- Copper beech leaves

— Crafting Tips —

Use peonies that are already opened and rounded for this arrangement; buds may not open once they are inserted in the floral foam. Cut the peony stems so that after they are inserted deep into the foam, the blossoms stand above the rim of the basket but not beyond the handle. Cut the stems on a sharp angle to enhance their ability to take in water. Don't use so many other flowers that they overwhelm the bouquet; allow the peonies to dominate.

1. Neatly tack ribbon around rim of basket with nylon thread, gathering ribbon a bit as you work.

2. Soak floral foam in water until saturated. With knife, cut foam to fit bowl, rounding off corners and edges.

3. Set bowl in center of basket. Insert peony leaves into floral foam to create a green base.

4. Cut peony stems on sharp angle. Insert stems into foam, angling them so that blossoms cover edge of basket.

5. Insert astilbes and bells of Ireland among peonies. Make sure their tips protrude above peonies.

6. Insert astilbe leaves and copper beech leaves along edge of basket. As needed, add water and replace wilted flowers.

Grass & Berry Wreath

A simple wreath of fresh grasses makes an attractive rustic table or wall accent. For added dimension and handsome visual appeal, this one is embellished with an intricate braid around its top, into which a chain of merry red berries has been incorporated. The grass along the outer rim is trimmed to neaten and define the shape of the wreath. As a plus, the grass and the berries will dry beautifully. If you like, gather your own materials on your next walk in the country.

What You'll Need

- **Flexible willow branch, about 13 inches long**
- **Spooled green floral wire, medium weight**
- **Armful tall, flexible grass**
- **Wire cutters**
- **Red berry sprigs**
- **Fine gold wire**
- **Scissors**

— *Crafting Tip* —

For braiding, you need flexible, soft grass. Cut it as long as you can, always leaving the roots behind.

1. Remove leaves from branch. Bend into 10-inch-diameter circle; secure with green wire. Make hanging hook with wire.

2. Bind thick clumps of grass to base by wrapping ends of grass with wire. Lay each clump over wire of previous one. Continue until wreath is covered with grass.

3. To make berry chain, divide berries into bunches of 2 to 3 berries each. Then attach them with gold wire to form a long chain, leaving about ¾ inch between the bunches.

4. Begin French braiding grass, working in opposite direction from which grass was bound. Pick up additional grass from each side as you braid.

5. Continue braiding, incorporating berry chain as you go.

6. Bind ends of braid together tightly with fine gold wire. Push wire and grass ends underneath beginning of braid.

7. Using scissors, trim grass evenly along outer rim to desired length.

Country Floral Arrangement

T his vibrant profusion of
daisies, anemones,
calendulas, and fragrant
mimosa looks and smells like
a sun-filled summer meadow.
The warm red, orange, and
yellow flowers are punctuated
by spots of bright white in a
lush arrangement that looks as
if you just gathered it in your
arms. Corkscrew willow
branches add twisty
contortions to the silhouette.
This wild-looking natural
display will bring the
countryside into your home.

What You'll Need

- 2 blocks floral foam
- Country-style container
- Knife
- Moss
- Pruning shears
- Thin corkscrew willow branches
- 10 stems yellow mimosa with leaves
- 15 white daisies
- 10 red Oriental poppies or wildflower anemones
- 8 orange calendulas
- Yellow satin ribbon, ⅛ inch wide (optional)
- Scissors

1. Place floral foam in container. Trim corners and edges on diagonal. Insert moss around edge of container.

2. Prune ends of willow branches on diagonal. Insert first branch in center of foam; evenly distribute remainder.

3. Insert mimosa stems angled toward center of foam to create dome shape that radiates from center out to edges.

4. Trim ends of all stems on an angle. Insert 2 to 3 daisies in center. Add rest of daisies, poppies, and calendulas.

5. Distribute flowers evenly, keeping rounded shape. Insert calendula stems deeper into foam to position as desired.

6. Check arrangement from all sides; adjust as necessary. If desired, cut ribbon into 6-inch lengths and tie to branches. Water daily; replace wilted flowers.

Figure-Eight Wreath

This cascading double wreath arrangement is eye-catching on many counts. Fiery orange Chinese lanterns and large magenta hydrangea blossoms glow against a deep-green moss background. The texture and color of the burlap bow are echoed in the peanuts scattered around the wreath. The short-lived hydrangea blossoms are strung as a garland and attached by wire so they can be replaced if you don't like how they look when they've dried. The two shapes are looped together by raffia.

What You'll Need

Heavy-gauge floral stem wire

Wire cutters

Green sheet moss

Spooled green floral wire

25 peanuts

15 beech leaves

20 Chinese lanterns

Hot glue gun, glue sticks

22 large hydrangea or phlox blossoms

Spooled fine gold wire

Burlap strip

Scissors

Raffia

1. From heavy wire, make 5- and 7-inch circles. You may need to use 2 lengths of wire. Twist ends to secure.

2. Attach moss around both forms by wrapping with spooled floral wire. Continue adding moss until circles are about 3 inches wide.

3. Position peanuts, beech leaves, and Chinese lanterns evenly around moss circles. Attach with hot glue.

4. Make hydrangea garlands by gently wrapping gold wire around bottom of each blossom, leaving a few inches of wire before wrapping next blossom. Make 2 garlands. If you like, string a few blossoms and Chinese lanterns to hang from bottom of wreath.

5. Drape a garland around each circle. Wrap garlands onto circles with gold wire to secure.

6. Make a bow from burlap strip. Twist wire around middle of bow, and attach bow to top of larger circle.

7. Securely join top of smaller circle to bottom of larger one with strands of raffia. Turn knotted ends to back.

Sunny Sunflower Arrangement

*A*lthough the star of this warm autumnal arrangement never grew in soil, the blend of authentic and artificial materials creates a beautiful whole. A glorious flower of summer, the sunflower can be exquisitely imitated in silk. With a smaller dried sunflower and real yarrow and tansy blossoms included, this arrangement will liven up even the darkest room. Bamboo, raffia, wheat, twigs, moss, and green apples complete the display.

— Crafting Tips —

The stalks of bamboo, sheaves of wheat, and the yarrow and tansy flowers are real, but they can be either fresh or dried. Stalks of bamboo add visual interest and structure to the piece. Using raffia and manila rope to tie on the components enhances the natural look.

1. If necessary, use wire cutters to shorten silk sunflower stem to 16 inches. Bend head down and leaves out to sides.

2. Place stalks of bamboo and sheaves of wheat along stem under flower head. With raffia, tie wheat and bamboo in place at top and bottom of stalks.

3. Lay dried sunflower below wheat heads. Add apples and yarrow, and space attractively. Cut a 16-inch length of rope. Attach flowers and apples with rope.

4. Adjust arrangement for balance and design. Below yarrow, tie raffia bow made of finger-thick skein.

5. Cut a 20-inch length of rope. Leaving a 6-inch tail, alternately tie bundles of twigs and clumps of moss to rope.

6. Attach tansy to tail of rope. Drape tied bundles of twigs and moss loosely over arrangement, with tansy at bottom.

Recipe Index

Craft Index

Notes

METRIC CONVERSION CHART

VOLUME MEASUREMENTS (dry)

$\frac{1}{8}$ teaspoon = 0.5 mL
$\frac{1}{4}$ teaspoon = 1 mL
$\frac{1}{2}$ teaspoon = 2 mL
$\frac{3}{4}$ teaspoon = 4 mL
1 teaspoon = 5 mL
1 tablespoon = 15 mL
2 tablespoons = 30 mL
$\frac{1}{4}$ cup = 60 mL
$\frac{1}{3}$ cup = 75 mL
$\frac{1}{2}$ cup = 125 mL
$\frac{2}{3}$ cup = 150 mL
$\frac{3}{4}$ cup = 175 mL
1 cup = 250 mL
2 cups = 1 pint = 500 mL
3 cups = 750 mL
4 cups = 1 quart = 1 L

VOLUME MEASUREMENTS (fluid)

1 fluid ounce (2 tablespoons) = 30 mL
4 fluid ounces ($\frac{1}{2}$ cup) = 125 mL
8 fluid ounces (1 cup) = 250 mL
12 fluid ounces ($1\frac{1}{2}$ cups) = 375 mL
16 fluid ounces (2 cups) = 500 mL

WEIGHTS (mass)

$\frac{1}{2}$ ounce = 15 g
1 ounce = 30 g
3 ounces = 90 g
4 ounces = 120 g
8 ounces = 225 g
10 ounces = 285 g
12 ounces = 360 g
16 ounces = 1 pound = 450 g

DIMENSIONS

$\frac{1}{16}$ inch = 2 mm
$\frac{1}{8}$ inch = 3 mm
$\frac{1}{4}$ inch = 6 mm
$\frac{1}{2}$ inch = 1.5 cm
$\frac{3}{4}$ inch = 2 cm
1 inch = 2.5 cm

OVEN TEMPERATURES

250°F = 120°C
275°F = 140°C
300°F = 150°C
325°F = 160°C
350°F = 180°C
375°F = 190°C
400°F = 200°C
425°F = 220°C
450°F = 230°C

BAKING PAN SIZES

Utensil	Size in Inches/Quarts	Metric Volume	Size in Centimeters
Baking or Cake Pan (square or rectangular)	8×8×2	2 L	20×20×5
	9×9×2	2.5 L	23×23×5
	12×8×2	3 L	30×20×5
	13×9×2	3.5 L	33×23×5
Loaf Pan	8×4×3	1.5 L	20×10×7
	9×5×3	2 L	23×13×7
Round Layer Cake Pan	8×1½	1.2 L	20×4
	9×1½	1.5 L	23×4
Pie Plate	8×1¼	750 mL	20×3
	9×1¼	1 L	23×3
Baking Dish or Casserole	1 quart	1 L	—
	1½ quart	1.5 L	—
	2 quart	2 L	—